THE UK BULLYING AND HATE CRIME HANDBOOK

Neville Evans

Bullied Publishing 2011

THE UK BULLYING AND HATE CRIME HANDBOOI

Copyright © 2011 Neville Evans

The right of Neville Evans to be identified as the Author of the work has been asserted by him in accordance with the copyright, Designs and Patents Act 1988.

First Edition

All rights reserved. No part of this publication may be produced, stored in a retrieval system, or transmitted, in any form or by any means, without the prior written permission of the publisher, nor be otherwise circulated in any form of binding or cover other than that which is published and without a similar condition being imposed on the subsequent purchaser.

The Authors views are personal and not the views of South Wales Police.

Published by Bullied Publishing 2011
137 New Road
Porthcawl
Bridgend
CF36 5DD
www.talkandsupport.co.uk
Cover Photograph: www.peterbritton.co.uk
Design: Neil Edwards (www.visucreative.co.uk)
With thanks to the Royal College of Psychiatrists, Mind and Jennifer Perry of e-victims.

ISBN 978-0-9561434-3-3

Printed in Great Britain by the MPG Books Group, Bodmin and King's Lynn

Contents

INTRODUCTION

Introduction

This book has been written for the person experiencing bullying or hate crime in all its forms. This book is intended as a tool for intervention and prevention of certain aspects of bullying and personal safety. If you have found yourself caught in the web of bullying or hate crime, this book along with the help of many professionals will guide you along the process of improving your circumstances.

I have written this book for the survivor of bullying and hate crime, however many professionals within certain fields may find it beneficial. Professionals working in the police service, social services, health, teaching professions, youth work and charitable organisations.

The purpose of this book is to give you clear safe advice, which addresses all your needs when confronted with dysfunctional bullying behaviors. When we are in a position of hostility and confrontation, we experience considerable stress on our mind and body. Stress places us in a position of disadvantage, we are unable to think clearly, rationally and our experience may project into the depths of despair. This book accounts for your personal experience as the author has seen and worked with many of you in many different settings.

The UK bullying and hate crime handbook is suitable for children aged 16yrs and over.

Within the following chapters the book will allow you to plan and consider your personal safety. The pitfalls of violence and confrontation can be planned for, many people have passed on their experiences of violence and this has culminated in a chapter specially dedicated to improving your safety.

Bullying and hate crime work on the emotional level. Depending on the severity of an experience, issues such as anxiety, depression, post-traumatic stress disorder, eating disorders and suicidal tendencies can manifest. A whole chapter has been dedicated to these issues, culminating in the exciting and scientifically proven research of mindfulness meditation.

Many agencies can help you, and the criminal justice system may be your first port of call. Within this system many agencies exist to support your ongoing needs. A whole chapter has been dedicated to the entire system, explaining the system from making a report to attending court.

There are many agencies within the UK that offer excellent services. An entire chapter is dedicated to the whole width of service across the UK. This overview will reduce the amount of time spent searching the internet and will match the correct service to your needs.

This book concentrates on the big four, hate crime, relationship bullying, cyber bullying and school bullying. These four types of bullying should not be viewed as separate entities; they cross over and affect one another.

Scientific studies from around the world, have concluded that bullying is a major world, health, peace, relationship and personal security problem. Bullying predisposes suffers to negative stress and negative emotions, such as anxiety and depression. The relationship between these states of mind and the body complex has been well researched within the past 10 years. Stress is significantly linked with negative emotions such as anger, hostility, anxiety and depression. There is evidence that suppressing emotional expression may play a role in high blood pressure as well as cancer. Depression is a distinctive feature and risk factor with regard to suicide and suicidal thoughts.

The link between domestic violence and relationship bullying is now starting to show a worrying trend. I have decided to cover this issue because domestic violence is possibly the worst form of bullying. I say this as it results in the majority of reported murders across the entire world.

Researchers tracing the development of violent behavior have found a link between teenage violence and domestic violence. A recent study from the latest issue of Personal Relationships shows that individuals who have experienced violence at an early age may have trouble adjusting to healthy, adult romantic relationships and are at a higher risk to experience marital difficulties. Domestic violence accounts for approximately 16% of violent crime within the UK. Recent American research has shown worrying trends involving teenage relationship bullying.

Bullying is an absolute horrible experience and one that can stay with you for the rest of your life. However it is our intention, to readdress the balance. Bullying disrupts the life force our communities, and is something that we need to understand in full. In writing this book, I can't imagine what some of you have gone through, but is my intention to help you minimise violent behavior, maintaining your peace and security at all times. After all what is life without peace and happiness?

The chapters of this book are designed to be used with one another. Don't just rely on one aspect of this book. The book has sections and exercises that are aimed at improving your understanding. Accessing support at the right time and considering a holistic approach to bullying and hate crime will allow you to change from a victim to a survivor.

Useful Contacts

Hate crime police officer ....

School bullying coordinator ....

Local hate crime charities ....

Local bullying charities ....

Samaritans ....

Counsellor ....

Doctors ....

Housing officer ....

Antisocial behaviour team ....

Security company ....

Sarc crisis worker ....

Solicitor ....

Victim care officer ....

Witness care officer ....

Victim support officer ....

Court ....

Social worker ....

Police officer ....

Therapist ....

Friends ....

Spiritual ....

Reporting incidents of bullying, harassment and hate crime

Incidents of Bullying should be reported to trusted members of your community.

You can report incidents to your school teachers, school bullying coordinators (a service usually provided by the council or voluntary sector), local police station, schools community police officers and police community support officers.

Relationship bullying where there is a threat, stalking and violence should always be reported to the police. Alternatively you can complete a specialist questionnaire and hand this to the police. You can access the v-dash (2010) risk identification checklist via the website **www.dashriskchecklist.co.uk**

Hate Crimes can be reported directly to the police or if you feel uncomfortable going to the police you can report them online. It might be a good idea to find out the number for your area – just Google 'non-emergency police number' along with where you live – and put it into your phone. Alternatively many of the agencies in the last chapter of this book have online reporting systems.

UK Online hate crime reporting

True Vision www.report-it.org.uk/home

Stop Hate UK is a charity that provides independent and confidential support to people affected by Hate Crime. They provide confidential Hate Crime reporting services in various areas of the UK, including a 24 hour helpline. Please check their list of areas carefully before calling.

Website: **www.stophateuk.org**

24 hour helpline: **0800 138 1625**

Scotland - **www.crimestoppersscotland-uk.org** or via your local police service

Wales - **www.saferwales.com**

Northern Ireland - **www.psni.police.uk**

1

**TOWARDS A NEW
UNDERSTANDING
OF BULLYING
AND HATE CRIME**

What is bullying and hate crime?

Bullying can be defined as the *willful, conscious desire to hurt, punish, control, threaten or frighten someone. Bullying involves repeated, targeted behavior.*

There are four main areas of bullying:

1 **Physical:** hitting, kicking, pushing and other forms of violence.

2 **Verbal:** teasing, taunting, threats and name calling.

3 **Indirect:** being ignored and left out, having rumours spread about you, making things up that can cause problems for you.

4 **Cyber:** is the term used to refer to bullying and harassment by use of technologies through means of email, instant messaging, text messages, blogs, mobile phones, pagers, and websites.

Other forms of bullying include:

❑ Having your possessions stolen by the use of violence or fear of violence

❑ Damaging your property

❑ Being forced to hand over money and/or possessions

❑ Threats

❑ Sending you offensive and/or abusive texts/emails

Hate crime is the umbrella term that describes a wide basis of dysfunctional behaviour.

A Hate Crime is any criminal offence which is perceived, by the victim or any other person, to be motivated by a hostility or prejudice based on a person's race or perceived race, religion or perceived religion, sexual orientation or perceived, person's disability or perceived disability, sexual orientation or perceived sexual orientation, transgender or perceived to be transgender.

Crimes include, assault, criminal damage, harassment, theft, public order offences and burglary.

A Hate incident is any non-crime incident which is perceived by the victim or any other person, to be motivated by a hostility or prejudice based on a person's race or perceived race, religion or perceived religion, sexual orientation or perceived, person's disability or perceived disability, sexual orientation or perceived sexual orientation, transgender or perceived to be transgender.

Incidents include anti-social behaviour for example: door knocking, noise nuisance, littering, dog fouling and graffiti. There are many other examples. Incidents of bullying can involve criminal acts, aspects of hate crime and antisocial behaviour. A standalone hate crime incident, may not always involve aspects of antisocial behaviour and bullying.

When does a hate crime become a bullying incident and vice versa?

A standalone hate crime incident, becomes a bullying incident when the perpetrator repeats their actions. The victim becomes a target.

Case study

I am 18 years old and I am a student at Bridgend Comprehensive School. I am currently studying three A levels and hope to go on to further education. My family are originally from Trinidad and I am of black ethnic origin. I attend school each week and I also have a Saturday and Sunday job at Somerfield Store, Bradford Road, Bridgend. I started work at the store six months ago. My duties include stacking shelves and working the tills. I work approximately 16 hours per week. The store employs local people and the majority of weekend workers are sixth formers. I work with some of my classmates. I work with the following friends: Jemma Edwards, Lucy Croft and Damien Bailey. We all work the same shifts and then go out with each other in the evenings. We all have a laugh and enjoy working together. At first the bullying was unnoticeable. I didn't think anything of it, and I just thought that John Cooper was a moody person. I have known John Cooper for six months. He works the same shifts as I do. Cooper is seven years older than me and has been working at the store since he left school. The harassment started three weeks ago. I have just started a relationship with Lucy Croft. We have known each other for years as we attend the same school. I recently asked Lucy to go out with me and Lucy agreed.

Within the first couple of days Lucy warned me about Cooper. Lucy told me that she had gone out with him for one year and that the relationship had ended three months ago. Although Cooper still works on the same shift as Lucy, he took the separation badly and there were a few problems between the two. Lucy wanted to keep our relationship a secret, however, people got to know about it and that's when the problems started.

> 'It appears that Lucy Croft was subjected to control and intimidation from John Cooper, this is clearly relationship bullying'

On Saturday the 10 August 2008 at 8pm I was at work at Somerfield's. I was directed to work behind the scenes in the dry goods warehouse by my manager Sue Evans. The dry goods area is a large warehouse that stores all the dry store goods. It has a centre aisle and has large shelving units either side. The store area measures thirty metres by thirty metres. It is room that is well lit. At this time I was stacking the clothes aisle with my friend Jemma Edwards.

What happened?

I was kneeling on the floor and placing clothes onto the shelves. Jemma was doing the same type of work. She was kneeling one metre away to my left-hand side. I was closer to the main aisle. There was no one to my right-hand side. We were talking about going out after work and Jemma was asking me about my relationship with Lucy. There was no one else in the warehouse. I could hear footsteps behind me and all of a sudden I felt a sharp pain to my head. I could hear a lot of screaming and I felt dazed and confused. I woke up and I saw Cooper standing above me. Cooper had a concerned look on his face and he was asking, "Are you alright? Are you alright?" I responded, "Yes, Yes." Jemma said to me, "You're bleeding. You have been cut." I could taste blood in my mouth and I placed my hand around the back of my head. I touched my head with my left hand and then looked at my hand. My hand was covered in blood. Cooper was in shock. His face was pale and he looked frightened. He said, "It was an accident, an accident." I said, "What happened?" Cooper said, "I was carrying some boxes and I slipped on a toffee wrapper and fell into you. I couldn't see you as the store room is dark". As Cooper said this Mrs Evans came into the warehouse. Mr Evans asked what had happened and I explained. My injury was cleaned and a bandage was wrapped around my head. I was OK -- a little shocked, but OK. I had a small cut to the back of my head. I didn't see what happened.

> At this point the perception of the victim is all important. The last comment 'I couldn't see you because the store room is dark'. Was this comment made because of the victim's ethnic origin? If the victim perceives this to be the case, then this matter would be recorded as a race hate incident.

The works canteen is situated in the centre of the store. It is a large room that has ample seating for 25 members of staff. The seating areas are divided into two rows. The main aisle runs down the middle of the two rows. The main entrance is situated directly opposite the serving area. To the right of the room are a number of whiteboards that are situated on the wall. The whiteboards contain staff information, items for sale and general notices. This room is the hub of the workforce and is a place where we all unwind.

What happened?

On Monday 12 August 2008 at 10 am I arrived at work and went to the male locker rooms. I got changed and put my works uniform on. I then walked from the locker rooms along the hall to the canteen. As I was walking to the canteen I saw my work colleague Diane Smith. I looked at Diane and said, "Good Morning." Diane replied and said, "Good Morning, Stripper!" As Diane said this she laughed and sniggered. I thought to myself, "How strange." I walked on and entered the canteen. I walked into the canteen and heard a loud wolf whistle. A group of female colleagues were sitting in the right hand far corner of the room. The women were sniggering and laughing among themselves. I was approximately ten metres away from the group. Standing next to the women and laughing with them was Cooper. I then stood at the end of the queue and waited to get served my cup of tea. To my horror I saw an A2 poster of a man completely naked. The man's body was superimposed and my head was placed on the man's body. The poster was very degrading as I was naked on the poster. At this point Cooper was standing five metres away from me. There were no obstructions in my view and the room was clearly lit. Cooper was the only person standing. He was wearing his works uniform. Cooper stood with stern authority; his chest was puffed up and looked directly at me. Cooper had a big grin on his face and was smiling at me. He pointed at me with his right arm and said, "Hey girls, he's a right stud." As Cooper said this he was making thrusting sexual movements with his hips. The women who were sitting next to him were laughing and pointing at my genitals. I was embarrassed and ashamed. I felt very upset and was totally humiliated. I turned around and walked out. I could hear all the staff laughing and this made me feel even worse.

> This tactic uses the group effect as a shield for a pattern of humiliating and degrading behaviour. There is no reference to the victim's ethnic identity. This is clearly bullying behaviour, however if the victim perceives it to be directed towards him as a result of his ethnic identity, then this incident will be recorded as a hate incident.

Incident 3

What happened?

I am the owner of a Nokia mobile phone operated by Easy Telecoms. The telephone number is 10987654321. On Wednesday 14 August 2008 I was at my friend's house watching a film. My friend's name is Jonathon Howe. At five past eight in the evening I received the following text message; "YOU ARE TREADING ON THIN ICE, IT'S GOING TO CRACK". I recognised the sender's number as Cooper's. I did not reply to this text message.

Whilst I was at my friend's house I accessed my email account on his laptop computer. I logged onto my account and I opened the first email. The email was sent by Cooper. The email read; "YOU ARE BEING WATCHED, BE CAREFUL, BE AFRAID".

Incident 4

I live at 20 John Street, Newtown. I live at this address with my parents. Our family home is a semi-detached property. The entrance to our home is attached to a small lean-to porch. The driveway measures ten metres and there is a small garden in front of the main entrance. John Street is a busy road and is the main trunk road that enters Newtown.

On Thursday 15 August 2008 at 8 am I got out of bed and got dressed. I went to the bathroom and brushed my teeth. I then walked across the landing and walked down the stairs. The stairs are situated directly opposite the front door. I looked at the door and I could see that a small parcel was situated on the floor. The parcel was situated next to a number of envelopes. I bent down and picked the parcel up. I brought the parcel closer to my line of sight. I looked at the address label; the parcel was addressed to me. I shook the parcel and felt some contents inside. The parcel was wrapped in brown wrapping paper and was light. The parcel measured approximately 20 cm by 20 cm. I began to open the parcel. I looked inside and saw that a book was contained within the wrapping. I pulled out the contents and read the title of the book. It read, "One hundred ways to kill yourself". I just reacted and threw the book on the floor. I felt physically sick.

> The last two incidents describe a course of conduct that amounts to harassment. This matter is now a crime. If the victim perceives it to be directed towards him as a result of his ethnic identity, then this incident will be recorded as a hate crime.

Incident 5

At this stage I am really afraid and I am constantly looking over my shoulder. I have stopped going to work and I am very nervous that the situation may escalate.

On Saturday 17 of August 2008 at 8 am I was walking along High Street. I walk to the Post Office each morning and get the papers for my family. High Street is an old Victorian street that has old houses situated either side of the road. The street has six or seven shops positioned in the centre of the village. The store where I work is not far away. It was a clear morning; the sun was shining and there were quite a lot of people about.

What Happened?

I made my way into the post office and purchased some papers and some milk. I know the girl behind the counter. Her name is Donna Mason. As I was standing in the cue I was talking to my old scout master Neil Evans. He asked me what I was doing with my life and I explained. I left the store at 8.10 am and walked out of the main entrance. I looked around; I could see a man standing next to his bicycle. The man was approximately five metres away from me. To my left Neil Evans walked away from the entrance. All of a sudden I felt a tap on my left shoulder. I turned my body to my left hand side and I saw Cooper standing a metre away. He was virtually on top of me. I felt anxious and afraid. His face was red and he was staring at me. His front teeth were showing and his jaw and face were shrivelled and tense. Within a split second he lunged his neck forward and spat at me. I could hear a "thump" sound as Cooper pursed his lips together and ejected saliva from his mouth. I closed my eyes and instantly placed my hands over my eyes. I couldn't see. The saliva was all over my nose and right eye. It felt disgusting, and was in shock.

Cooper was shouting at me. He pointed at me with his left fore finger. His hand was moving in a stabbing motion and he shouted the words, "YOU'RE HAVING IT BLACK BOY, YOU'RE HAVING IT BLACK BOY." As Cooper said these words his face became redder, and was snarled and angry. Cooper's right hand was clenched into a fist. He was stamping his feet on the floor at the same time. His chest was inflated and his arms were splayed out. I could see the veins in his neck protruding and his upper body was tense and muscular. All of a sudden he pulled his right arm backwards and stepped forward in a swinging motion. Simultaneously he threw a full body hook punch. I saw a flash. I remember feeling pain to my head. I lost consciousness and woke up on the floor. I could see and hear a number of voices. Words and noises were swirling around me. Cooper had left the area. I touched my lower lip and I could feel a protruding lump. My right fore finger was covered in blood. I had sustained the following injuries: two dislodged lower front teeth, bruised and swollen lower mouth, including my gums and skin.

> This last incident is clearly a hate crime. Overall the entire series of events include bullying, harassment, relationship bullying and hate crime. These terms cross one another and sometimes serve to confuse people. Overall these terms describe varying levels of dysfunctional behaviour.

2

RELATIONSHIP
BULLYING

Is your relationship healthy?

Look at the two columns below - if you find yourself picking more from the right hand side than the left - it could be time to think.

Healthy	Un – Healthy
❑ Have fun together	❑ Gets extremely jealous
❑ Trust each other	❑ Puts the other down by calling names
❑ Always feel safe with each other	❑ Making the other feel bad about him or herself
❑ Each enjoy spending time separately, with your own friends, as well as with each other's friends	❑ Yells at the other person
❑ Support each other's individual goals in life, like getting a job or going to university.	❑ Doesn't listen when the other talks
	❑ Frequently criticizes the other's friends or family
❑ Respect each other's opinions, even when they are different	❑ Has ever threatened to hurt the other or commit suicide if they leave
❑ Solve conflicts without putting each other down, swearing at each other or making threats	❑ Cheats or threatens to cheat
	❑ Tells the other how to dress
❑ Both accept responsibility for your actions	❑ Has ever grabbed, pushed, hit, or physically hurt the other
❑ Are faithful to each other Both say sorry when you're wrong	❑ Blames the other for your own behavior e.g "if you hadn't wound me up, I wouldn't have…"
❑ Have equal decision-making power about what you do in your relationship	❑ Embarrasses or humiliates the other
	❑ Smashes, throws, or destroys things
❑ Each control your own money	❑ Tries to keep the other from having a job or furthering his/her education
❑ Are proud to be with each other	❑ Makes all decisions about what you do
❑ Encourage each other's interests	
❑ Have some privacy - your letters, diary, personal phone calls are respected as your own	❑ Tries to make you feel as though everything is your fault.
	❑ Goes back on promises
❑ Have close friends & family who like the other person and are happy about your relationship	❑ Pressures the other for sex
	❑ Acts controlling or possessive – like they own you
❑ Never feel like you're pressured for sex	❑ Uses alcohol /drugs as excuse for hurtful behavior
❑ Communicate about sex, if your relationship is sexual	❑ Ignores or withholds affection to punish the other
❑ Allow each other "space" when you need it	❑ Depends completely on the other to meet social or emotional needs
❑ Always treat each other with respect	

Abuse is about control.

Abusers often feel little control over other aspects of their lives, so they attempt to control their partner in order to ease this insecurity.

Abuse may follow a pattern.

Abusers may have once been a victim. Anger and violence may seem like a normal way to express anger and frustration.

The Excuse	Your Response
"I was having a bad day."	"Hurting or making someone else feel badly will never solve your problems or improve your day."
"It's not abuse."	"You hurt your boy/girlfriend. It is abuse."
"My girl/boyfriend got me upset/angry, etc."	"No matter how someone makes you feel, it's up to YOU to choose how to react."
"It was a one-time thing. It won't happen again."	"Once is too many times to abuse someone."
"My boy/girlfriend deserved it."	"No one deserves to be abused - for any reason."
"I was drunk/high. Drugs made me do it."	"Stop blaming other things. It doesn't matter what you were on. Nothing can force you to act a certain way - it is a choice you make."
"I didn't mean to hurt her/him."	"Well, you did. And that's abuse."

Abusers use excuses like these to rationalize their behavior. Pay especially close attention to the suggested responses if you recognize the excuses. The responses send a signal that you do not accept the excuse:

Trick or Treat?

We are taught that gifts and presents are thoughtful and expressions of love, friendship or respect. We are also taught that a gift is a "way to ask for forgiveness" and the more expensive or rare or sentimental the gift, the more forgiveness it can get in return.

How many of us would soften after a quarrel if their boyfriend or girlfriend brought them a gift or present the next day? We would probably accept the present as an apology, forgive our partner and hope that we wouldn't fall out again.

But what if it keeps happening? What if the arguments are getting worse, even physical?

Do we accept the gifts as a treat, that means that your boyfriend or girlfriend is sorry, or do we look on them as a trick to keep you in a relationship with them. The difficult part is that the gifts and presents can be really nice to get, it is a something that says, "I was thinking about you." But it doesn't mean "I acknowledge, understand and take responsibility for what I've done."

If you recognize that you may be given gifts as a way of keeping you with your girlfriend or boyfriend it could mean that you are in an abusive relationship. Trick or treat? If this had made you think about your own relationship, then you probably already know.

Sexual Cyber bullying 'Think before you send' - Sexting

What is sexting?

Most of you have a mobile phone and use it to keep in touch with family and friends, and especially your girlfriend or boyfriend. It is now so easy to send pictures instantly via emails and texts that there are more and more instances of young people sending sexual images of themselves to each other without considering what could happen. This is known as sexting.

What are the risks?

Once you've sent a sexy text or image, it's gone and you will have no control over who sees it after that. It could be forwarded time and time again making your supposedly personal pictures or video public, it could end up published on the internet and end up anywhere in the world and in the hands of peadophiles. Of course this would be highly embarrassing for you and could damage your other relationships with your family and friends and even future employment.

The emotions involved in sexting are just as real as with any other kind of sex and if you're sexting with someone other than your regular partner you may feel guilty and if your regular partner finds out, they could feel hurt and betrayed and it could end your relationship. You may be in love now and believe that your partner would never hurt you, but what if you break up? The images could be used to blackmail you, or harass you. a good way to monitor what pics that you send to friends and partners is to think that you wouldnt mind if it did go public.

You should also be aware that if you're caught with nude pictures of anyone under 18, you could be prosecuted and end up on the sex offenders register. If you receive any sexts it is probably a good idea to delete them as quickly as you can, you may lose your phone or it could get stolen and the images could be posted on any social media site for a joke, or once again used to blackmail you.

To avoid trouble with the law which includes getting your partner in trouble it is good advice that you don't send nude pictures or video of yourself until you're over 18!

Sexual Abuse

Examples:

- ❑ Unwanted kissing or touching.
- ❑ Forcing someone to go further sexually than he or she wants to.
- ❑ Unwanted rough or violent sexual activity.
- ❑ Not letting someone use birth control.
- ❑ Not letting someone use protection against sexually transmitted diseases.
- ❑ Rape.

Any intentional behavior that is unwanted or interferes with the other girlfriend/boyfriend's right to say "no".

Sexual Assault Referral Centre

If you have been raped or sexually assaulted, the local authority will usually have a SARC within it's boundaries. For access to this service you could contact the police, women's aid or NHS direct.

A SARC is a one stop location where female and male victims of rape and serious sexual assault can receive medical care and counselling, and have the opportunity to assist the police investigation, including undergoing a forensic examination.

What can a SARC do?

- ❑ Crisis workers to support you after rape and sexual assault.
- ❑ Immediate on-site access to emergency contraception and drugs to prevent sexually transmitted infections including HIV.
- ❑ Integral follow-up services including psycho-social support/counselling, sexual health, and support throughout the criminal justice process.
- ❑ A dedicated, forensically secure facility integrated with hospital services.
- ❑ Availability of forensic examination 24 hours a day, within 4 hours in cases of immediate need.
- ❑ Facilities for self-referrals, including the opportunity to have a forensic examination and for the results to be stored or to be used anonymously. You don't necessarily have to involve the police.
- ❑ Choice of gender of doctor/forensic medical examiner/appropriately trained Sexual Assault Nurse Examiner. All examiners should be supervised by doctors trained and experienced in sexual assault forensic examination, who can provide interpretation of injuries for criminal justice purposes and ensure the highest standard of forensic examination.

Personal Safety

In an abusive relationship your personal safety is at risk. The abuser's personality is unpredictable at first, however, the longer you stay, the more predictable it may become. It is important to try and see a pattern; what triggers the abuser to act in a particular way. In essence this form of personal flexibility (you are adapting to the abuser's outbursts) becomes a subtle form of control (you are changing your behaviour because of abusive behaviour). Please don't become stubborn. Remember planning your safety allows you to have an element of flexibility and control. You are managing an abusive situation and successfully stopping more physical abuse.

Safety plans need to be considered as if you were planning for a fire alarm. Read through each plan and think about the various places where abuse may happen, spot the potential hazards. Move to different areas of your home and try and imagine what you would do if you were attacked. Think about other scenarios, for example, walking home from a night out or a friends house. Visualise the steps that you would take and the things that you would do. This allows it to be an automatic response if the inevitable happens.

Safety Planning in an abusive relationship

Recognising confrontation, situational awareness

Ask the following questions: Where is your partner? What room are you in? What state of mind are they in?

The stare

The abuser will hold a stare across the room, and is looking for you to catch his/her gaze. This stage of awareness is an opportunity for you to avoid confrontation. Do not make it obvious but keep a watch over the abuser.

The question

If you have been indecisive and have not avoided the abuser, you are ready for the next stage of confrontation. Your abuser is going to project feelings of inadequacy onto you and make you the problem. They will say, "Have You Got A Problem With Me?". What they are really saying is, "I am insecure, and I have a problem with you". Be aware that at this stage the abuser has already planned to attack you. The abuser may attack you verbally or physically, depending on the circumstances.

The body language

Body language will change as the situation escalates. Even at the first stage look for the vital signs of body language that demonstrates violence. Communication is mostly through body language. They will get closer to you. The following description is equally applicable to men and women. Your abuser's chest will be inflated like a balloon, and arms will puff outwards like a bird. They will stand tall and appear robotic. When talking they will use hands and point in a stabbing motion. The face will redden, eyes will bulge, and teeth may show. The jaw will tighten and they will appear bigger. The abuser will constantly look around and may stamp the floor.

The provocation

Here it becomes increasingly tense. The abuser will mutter words like, "Yeah, yeah, so, so". At this stage it will be almost impossible to communicate with them. What the abuser is doing is target picking. The provocation can last some time depending on the abuser. A violent abuser will build up to this stage in a matter of split seconds. They will also swear at you.

The Attack

The distance between you and the abuser will shorten and they may look for an opportunity to attack. This will depend your own body language. The majority of attackers are right-handed and right-footed. Do you know if your abuser is right or left-handed? In most cases your abuser is going to throw a right-hand hooking punch to the head. This isn't always the case as some like to grab and pull your hair.

What Can I Do About It?

You cannot change an abuser, only an abuser can do that. You have to adapt to the abuser's behaviour and make quick decisions.

Situational Awareness

Keep your head up and look around you, and every now and again look behind you. Gather information, and use your eyes and ears. Anticipate problems before they arise. Think Safety PLAN. Think VULNERABILITY.

Plan and Prepare

Now that I have given an explanation of the stages of a violent confrontation, consider the following safety planning advice.

- ❑ Don't drink alcohol together as the probability of a violent attack increases. If he or she insists, try and pour some lemonade into your drink. Alcohol reduces your ability to run, defend yourself and escape.

- ❑ You cannot reason with a drunk person. Don't try to tell them what to do. If they are starting to pick on you then make the decision for them and get out of their way.

- ❑ Keep them fed and watered. Why on earth would someone tell me to do this? Simply; physiological stress has a major impact on the brain. If someone has the abusing personality and they are hungry and drunk, then probability of violence increases ten fold. If they are drinking alcohol make sure they eat something too. It will stop them from getting really drunk. It may help you.

- ❑ Plan your safety around sporting events. If he/she is a sporting fan, consider when his/her team are playing. When the abuser's team wins, the probability of violence, believe it or not increases. If he/she is going drinking all day with friends, plan to stay with a family member or close friend.

- ❑ Hide money in your shoes. You may need money to order a taxi.

- ❑ Consider purchasing a Howsar quick lock. This handy lock will give you time to get away. The portable lock allows you to lock a door in a short amount of time. Employ a diversionary tactic first "I am putting some make up on or I am getting you a beer from the fridge". Lock the escape door and get out of the house.

- ❑ Keep your mobile on you at all times and make sure it has sufficient credit. You can get a prefix security number for your phone. For example if you press and hold 3, then your mobile will ring 999 or a security. Another good idea, is to silently ring 999, keep the phone off the receiver and if he gets near to you start shouting. Police services in the UK will respond immediately to such incidents.

The stare

It is absolutely normal to avoid confrontation and aggression - avoid the abuser and leave the area. There are many factors to consider at this stage. Is he or she bigger and more aggressive than you? Has he or she been drinking alcohol? Does they have a history of violence? Prepare yourself if your sixth sense starts to answer "yes" to these questions. Do you have a panic alarm handy? Where are you going to run?

Consider trickery

The abuser may try and entice you into what is called a deceptive attack. What they will do is ask a stupid question and then attack you. (This is a technique that distracts and confuses you).

The question

"HAVE YOU GOT A PROBLEM WITH ME?"

If your bully comes close then step away, keep your hands up, and turn your palms outwards. Stand at a 45 degree angle. Tuck your chin in and talk at a distance. Move side to side when talking to them. Say to them firmly; *"NO, I DON'T WANT TROUBLE. I DON'T WANT TO FIGHT."* Don't turn your back on them and keep to the wall. Appear to give in to them. Remember that by complying with their rules you are giving them a sense of control. You are also playing for time and preparing to respond.

The body language

Appear non-confrontational and keep your hands and palms facing outwards. This is a ploy as it tells the abuser you are not willing to fight and gives them a sense of power. Tell them what they want to hear and keep on saying it even if it is, "I am sorry, I am sorry". Give them power. Many women who have been beaten by their partners sometimes say it is best to say very little. By saying very little you do not add to the problem (in his or her mind). Every case is different and you will be the best person to decide.

The provocation

Do not argue and try to remain calm. Keep well away from them. They are dangerous but you have options: you can run away, you can activate your panic alarm or you can defend yourself.

During a violent incident men and women cannot always avoid violent incidents. However, in order to increase your safety, here are some things you can do:

❑   remind yourself that you have an Emergency Escape Plan, and go over it in your mind;

- never retaliate – research shows that the likelihood of further aggravated violence increases. Retaliation gives the abuser a licence to use more violence. If they are especially vindictive, they will call the police and tell them that they have been assaulted;

- start to position yourself to get out quickly or near a phone so you can call 999, if necessary;

- try to move to a space where the risk is the lowest (try to avoid arguments in the bathroom, garage, kitchen, near weapons, or in rooms without access to an outside door);

- use your judgement and intuition – if the situation is very serious, you can agree with your partner or give him/her what he/she wants to calm him/her down. You have to protect yourself until you are out of danger;

The attack

If you are getting attacked keep moving away from them. Cover your face and try and protect yourself. Do not let them get too close. Keep on shouting, *"HELP, HELP, STOP, and STOP."*

New Year, New start - Staying safe when breaking up.

Its the start of a brand new year, and a time that we reflect on our lives and may want to make changes. You may have realised that you are in an unhealthy relationship and want to end it.

Breaking up is never easy and it can be especially difficult if you are in an abusive relationship. You may be feeling very confused about your girlfriend or boyfriend. Some of the reasons that you may find it difficult to end your relationship may be:
Fear: You might be scared that your boyfriend or girlfriend will hurt you if you try to break up with them, they may even threaten to hurt family members or hurt themselves.

Love: You may still have feelings for your boyfriend or girlfriend, you have shared good times together he or she is loving and caring towards you (sometimes).

Shame: It's not easy to admit that your relationship with your boyfriend or girlfriend isnt as happy as you may have projected to your friends and family. It can be embarrassing to let the people closest to you know what you have been subjected to.

Worry: You may be worried how your friends may react, they may not believe you, they may blame you. You may worry that your parents will want to get involved and either call the police or "sort" your partner out themselves.

One of an abuser's main tactics is CONTROL and because you have decided to take control and end your relationship, it not only breaks the control an abuser has over you but also may make him or her feel powerless and out of control this can make them act in a violent and desperate manner, therefore it is a good idea to have a safety plan to keep yourself safe.

Inform parents and friends that you are ending the relationship. In case something should happen, your parents and friends should know that you are planning to break up with your partner. It is also likely that your ex will try to make contact with you, and family members and or friends can be the first line of defense in helping you to avoid your abuser.

Break up in a public space. If you decide to end the relationship face to face, meet with the person in a public space, tell friends and family what you are going to do, where you will be and make sure that you have your mobile phone with you.

End the relationship by phone or email. If you are really concerned for your safety, do not end the relationship in person, it may seem cruel or cowardly but your safety comes first.

After the break up your partner may try and get in touch with you, you must try and remain strong as you may also be missing them too, and the routine and life that you used to have with them. You will need to send an emphatic message that the relationship is over and that they no longer have control over you or your actions.

Discourage Communication: Do not return phone calls, text messages, instant messages, or emails. Delete them as your friend on any social network that you belong to. Do not let your ex into your home if they show up unexpectedly.

Stalking

After your relationship has ended a critical period usually follows. This is when emotions are heightened and there is a period of loss that both experience. There may be a period of pestering, it may be that your ex-partner is actually stalking you. If you are being stalked you need to contact the police immediately. You are in particular danger if your ex-partner has a problem with alcohol or drug abuse. Stalking is a serious matter, if you feel frightened you must tell the police about your fears. If you see your ex-partner more than two occasions within a week, make that phone call. Leave the area immediately and do not attempt to speak to the abuser.

Findings from the British Crime Survey 2004 show that every year in the UK 1.2 million women and 900,000 men are victims of harassment. The National Stalking Helpline provides practical advice and information to anybody who is currently or has previously been affected by harassment or stalking.

When should I contact the National Stalking Helpline?

❑ Are you or someone you know being made to feel harassed or intimidated by the behaviour of another person?

❑ Are you unsure what can be done about this person's behaviour?

- [ ] Do you feel that you, your friend or family member are at risk of emotional or physical harm?

- [ ] Do you think this person has or will damage personal property?

- [ ] Do you feel you cannot go directly to the police about this behaviour?

If you answered 'yes' to any of these questions and require advice or

information, please call 0300 636 0300

If you think you are a victim of stalking then you may want to complete a risk assessment tool called a VS DASH.

The VS DASH (Victim Stalking) has been specifically designed for stalking victims to fill in themselves. It is recommended that if you decide to report what has been happening to the police, you take the completed VS DASH with you and show it to a police officer.

www.dashriskchecklist.co.uk

Record all incidents of harassment. The next chapter 'Writing about your experiences' will help you write a bullying and harassment diary.
Staying safe after breaking up.

- [ ] If you have fixed appointments that your partner is aware of, change the time and location.

- [ ] Your mobile phone could be "tracked"; this is only supposed to happen if you have given your permission, but if your partner has had access to your mobile phone, he could have sent a consenting message purporting to come from you. If you think this could be the case, you should contact the company providing the tracking facility and withdraw your permission; or if you are in any doubt, change your phone.

- [ ] Never answer the door unless you know who is the other side.

- [ ] Keep to main routes and avoid places of darkness. Stick to well lit and busy areas. Plan your route and stick to areas where there is CCTV.

- [ ] Try and vary your times and locations when travelling.

- [ ] When you leave your home, tell someone where you are going, when you will be returning and how you can be contacted. Leave a timetable of your likely whereabouts with loved ones.

- [ ] Carry a mobile phone and make sure it has enough credit on it.

- [ ] Shout 'fire' rather than 'help' as it can get more results. If he starts to chase you, bang on every door possible in the street and draw attention to yourself.

- [ ] Try and use the mirrors of cars and reflections of shop windows -- that way you can see what is behind you.

- ❏ When out walking, you should avoid using your mobile phone or texting on the go. This distraction can stop you from being aware of your surroundings. Similarly listening to your iPod whilst walking can limit your awareness.

- ❏ Do not get drunk, you will not be able to think clearly and act decisively.

- ❏ Avoid dark gloomy places, subways, bridges, open fields and dark lanes. Never take a short cut.

The person that you have been dating had probably become a huge part of your life. You might have seen more of them than your friends and family. Being scared about feeling lonely after the break up is normal. Make sure that you talk to friends and try to find activities to fill the new time that you have. It will take some time but eventually you will realise that its the best thing that you ever did and you will suddenly find that you are not living a life of fear.

Relationship Abuse and the link with hate crime

The victims of LGBT domestic abuse may experience all of the above behaviours. However there are a number of subtle differences. These include: the threat of 'outing' one's sexual orientation to people who don't know or understand LGBT issues. The threat may include divulging personal information to close family members, work colleagues, religious groups, extremist groups etc. The threat of using this information acts as a way of controlling their victim. This type of behaviour is also known as blackmail.

Broken Rainbow
03009995428 Help line for LGBT people experiencing relationship violence.
www.broken-rainbow.org.uk

24-hour National Domestic Violence Helpline	**0808 2000 247**
Wales Domestic Abuse Helpline	**0808 80 10 800**
England Domestic Abuse Helpline	**0808 2000 247**
Scottish Domestic Abuse Helpline	**0800 027 1234**
Northern Ireland Domestic Abuse Helpline	**0800 917 1414**

3

WRITING ABOUT OUR EXPERIENCES

Creating a bullying diary

You must remember the old saying, "Sticks and stones will break my bones, but names will never hurt me". So why do words hurt so much and, how do we minimise those hurtful words?

To understand what a word is we first have to understand what an emotion is. Emotions and feelings are the same thing. You can't touch them. You can't see them. They are hard to describe, but you can definitely feel them. The clue is in the word e-motion. Motion means to move and that is exactly what your emotions do. Close your eyes and think of a time when someone made you feel really emotional. Try and relive that moment. Imagine what you were feeling and concentrate on the inner feeling.

Does the following description bear some reality? I feel crazy, fiery, bursting, red hot, tense, agitated, and aggressive. What we are really describing is an inner vibration. Certain emotions vibrate more than others and move us to act in certain ways. Think of emotions as constructive or destructive. Anger is a destructive emotion. It causes more problems, blocks understanding and leads to frustration. Compassion is a constructive emotion it aids communication, builds trust and helps you.

Words start from the inner level of someone who is speaking. They begin as vibrating emotions; when the person talks his voice box changes those vibrations into sounds. Sound at the scientific level is a series of waves and waves are oscillating vibrations. When a bully uses harsh words with real intent behind them, it really sends a clear message. What is happening is that those words communicate on an emotional level because those words invoke a greater level of vibration within you.

When somebody says, "They are only words. Ignore it", they are really saying, "I don't want to help." Words and the associated emotion behind their meaning are very destructive. In order to prevent words from piercing our armour, we first have to understand our emotions. The word "understand" literally means to stand under something. If you analyse and stand under something you look at it in a different light.

How do I recognise my emotions?

Emotions cannot be scientifically measured. However, scientists can measure the effect of emotions by measuring their effect on the body. For example fear can increase your heart rate, adrenaline or blood pressure. The only scientific tool that has been developed to measure real emotions is called the "human being". You can do it easily, all you need to do is find a quiet place, sit and relax. If you have had a hard day sit down and find a breathing space for 15 minutes. If you have decided that you are angry, breath deeply and concentrate on the inner feeling. Re-visit the experiences that made you feel angry and hold the feeling of anger in your mind. In your mind compare the feeling of anger with the "tick-tock" of an old-fashioned alarm clock. Give the emotion of anger a numerical value. Breathe deeply, inhaling for four seconds and exhaling for four seconds. Visualise with time; the alarm clock slowing and the inner vibration easing.

When we learn to play a musical instrument we attribute a particular sound or vibration with a particular note. A skilled musician will be able to listen to the sound and tell you what the note is. In the same way feelings (inner vibrations) become the sounds and you become the musician. You can now give each emotion a name and recognise how it feels.

This very simple exercise allows you to tune in with how you are feeling. I have seen thousands of people in distress over the years. When people are in distress they find it difficult to communicate their feelings. Emotions are generally described using words and this is where we fall down. Emotions are not words.

What emotions will I be feeling?

The Emotion of Humiliation - disgraced, defeated, alienated

When you have been humiliated you feel like you want to crawl into a cave and disappear. Humiliation means to inform other people about your weaknesses or faults and broadcast those facts to many people. The effect is of a silent paranoia or public hysteria. Your ego takes a battering and you feel very small indeed. It can be a very powerful tool if used against someone in a bullying situation.

The Opposite of Humiliation - confident, self-assured

Focus on the feeling of humiliation for ten minutes in a quiet room. Visualise the feeling of humiliation vibrating inside your heart. How fast does the feeling vibrate? Give this emotion a number.

The Emotion of Anger - mad, bitter, irritated, resentful

When you feel angry you lose present control and can act in many different ways. Anger is a turbulent thunderous mind that wants to explode.

The Opposite of Anger - loving, friendly, peaceful, agreeable

The Emotion of Fear – scared, frightened, worried, nervous

When you feel fearful you are worried that you may come to some harm. Fear can be in the physical sense in that you are concerned that you may be injured.

Psychological fear is a fear that your status or identity may be threatened.

The Opposite of Fear - confident, trusting, hopeful

The Emotion of Hurt - distress, upset, tearful, sad

When we are hurt by someone we feel that our ideas were not listened to and that our opinions do not count. We value our personal contribution and like to feel valued and part of the team. Hurt is a feeling that we can make worse by constantly reminding ourselves of the hurtful situations that we have encountered in the past.

The Opposite of Hurt – relieved, comforted, cheerful, glad

The Emotion of Disgust – repelled, put off by

When we are disgusted, we feel that avoidance is the only answer. Not only do we feel that we want to avoid, but disgust leaves a lingering and lasting bad feeling towards another.

The Opposite of Disgust – affectionate, fond of, impressed

> By spending time and considering our emotional responses to bullying and hate incidents, we create the opportunity to express ourselves with clarity and accuracy and this process will certainly help our writing ability. After an incident, take some time to cool off and then begin your diary entry.

Many people are unaware of the types of behaviour and actions that constitute abuse. We sometimes minimise behaviour saying it was just an argument or a "one off". Excuses are made for someone's behaviour, and over the months and years this behaviour can serve to delude us into thinking that it is normal. It isn't normal behaviour, and the effects are far reaching. Whilst we experience trauma our mind can play tricks with us, and serve to mask our traumatic experiences. When exposed to traumatic experiences our subconscious mind will blot out the actual experience. However the devastating experience is still held in our subconscious mind.

We are unaware of how our experience starts to impact on our everyday

experiences, for example, we may get flash backs, we may feel we cannot remember certain dates and times, we may feel upset and scared for no apparent reason. If you have come to the stage whereby you have asked for help from the legal profession then it will come to the stage where you are asked to provide a statement. In your present capacity it may become difficult to remember the actual events that have occurred. Whatever stage you are at it is important to write about your experiences. You may not like to write you may feel that you wish to draw instead.

Writing about your experiences has many benefits including:

❑   Identifying a pattern to your abuser's violent behaviour, and seeing the trigger events that lead to violence.

❏ Expressing yourself in a therapeutic sense.

❏ Seeing the scale of abuse and confirming it isn't your fault.

❏ When you are ready this information could help you when you contact the police or a solicitor.

Writing a personal diary

Start your diary with the time and date of the incident. Write about the day; something that will trigger your memory. For example was it someone's birthday or a recognised holiday? It doesn't matter what you write about. It is only there to help you remember.

Make some notes before writing your diary. When you make your notes break each aspect of the incident into small sections. Put each section into small circles and apply the following questions: who, what, why, where, when, and how. Once you have answered each question move onto the next section. The smaller you break each part down the more detailed your diary will become. Once you have a plan stand back and leave it alone for a couple of hours. Return to your notes after you have been refreshed and repeat the entire process again. Now write your story in small simple sentences. Remember to use descriptive words and do not leave any details out.

Include the following information in your personal diary:

❏ **Amount of time** (when the incident started and finished)

❏ **Distance** (how far you were away from the abuser?)

❏ **Visibility** (what were the lighting conditions like; was it night or day; how well you could see the abuser?)

❏ **Obstructions** (was there anything obstructing your view?)

❏ **Known or seen before** (how do you know the abuser)

Posters / graffiti

In certain circumstances abusers may publicise malicious words about you. They may spray graffiti outside your home, on your property or publicise something personal via a poster. Take a picture of the poster with your digital camera. Ask someone else to witness the position of the poster and ask the witness to sign their name on the bottom right hand corner. Make sure you include the time and date. Remove the picture carefully. Make sure you remove it wearing gloves and place it in a large envelope. Do not touch the poster or show it to anybody else. Record the time and date you removed the poster and sign the envelope accordingly. Write a dairy entry about the poster. You can draw diagrams or use maps/plans in order to illustrate your point of view.

Text message's

If you have received an abusive text message there are many things you can do. Firstly do not respond to the text message. Write out the text message on a piece of paper, sign and date it. It should read something like this:

On Wednesday 14 August at 2200 hours I received a text message from the mobile number 12345678910. I know this to be ****** phone. It was sent to my phone number 10987654321.

This mobile phone is owned by me and I am an Easy Telecoms customer. The text message said, "YOU ARE TREADING ON THIN ICE, IT'S GOING TO CRACK". I did not reply to this message.

Repeat the procedure with each text message. Ask a witness to read the messages and ask them to sign each written diary entry. Save each message on your phone's SIM card. Remove the SIM card and keep it for safe keeping. Purchase a new SIM card and consider changing your mobile phone number. You also need to evidence how you obtained your abuser's mobile phone number. Include when and where you exchanged mobile phone numbers.

Email

Save the email on your computer or on a removable memory stick or CD. Print the email using your computer and show it to a witness. Write the date and time on the printout and sign the document. Keep the email somewhere safe and hand it to the person dealing with your case at the earliest possible time. Make a diary entry of what happened; include how you felt when you opened the email. Do not respond to abusive emails.

Package's

If your abuser sends you a package in the post try to resist handling the item as you may lose vital forensic evidence. Typically old photographs and damaged personal items have been sent in the post. Do not let anyone else touch the item. Ring the police immediately and pass the item to the police. You could also take a photograph of the item - specifically where you found it. Write about this incident in your personal diary.

Being spat at

If someone has spat at you, you need to preserve the evidence. If you do remove it keep the tissue that has the saliva on it. Place the saliva in a brown bag and seal it. Record on the bag who spat at you, the time and date. You could take a photograph of the saliva on your face. This is not always practical as the first thing you want to do is remove it.

Photographs

If you have been assaulted make sure you take photographs of your injuries after the incident. The police may also take photographs of your injuries. You could consider taking photographs a number of days later, as bruising and swelling tend to show more prominently after a few days. If you take digital photographs be sure to save the photographs on a CD-ROM or memory stick. Keep this information safe. Try and make sure that you record the time and date of when and where the photographs were taken. If a friend has witnessed your injuries, again, record the time and date when they saw you. Record who the witnesses are.

Mobile phone voice recording

If you have received an abusive phone message there are many things you can do. Firstly do not respond to the message. Write out the message on a piece of paper, sign and date it. Ask a witness to listen to the message and ask them to sign your diary and confirm that this message was abusive. Speak to someone who can help you save the message. Messages can be saved on a portable recording device such as a dictaphone. You could speak to your phone provider about changing your telephone number.

Computer messages

Copy any postings or IM chats by pressing the 'Alt' and 'Prt Sc – SysRq' or 'Printscreen' keys together, a Windows PC will take a copy of what is on your screen. Open up a new document and paste the image into it, add the time and date of the incident and also make sure you include the incident in your log. Today's cyber world involves the use of social networking sites. If you are receiving abusive messages via a site, again, don't respond and save the messages. It is advisable to avoid this type of communication until matters have settled down.

Your home

If your abuser has ransacked your home and assaulted you, you may have to call the police. Before the police arrive do not clean up the mess, but leave everything as it is. You may want to take photographs of the damage. If there is blood on the floor or in a room do not clean it up. This type of evidence is best photographed.

Being assaulted

If you have been assaulted you need to get medical treatment and get your injuries medically recorded. Whilst at the doctor's or hospital ask for the name of the person treating you and record this information in your diary.

Stalking

If you are being watched and followed you really need to consider your personal safety. Revert back to the chapter "Personal Safety" for tips and advice. Always carry a mobile phone or a small digital camera. Do not overtly take photographs of the abuser. This may act as a catalyst for an escalation of violence. Look around your environment. Are there any witnesses who saw your abuser? Is there any CCTV at the location?

Letters of apology

Many abusers will try and write letters and offer reasons why they have hurt you. Keep these letters safe and enter a record of these letters in your personal diary.

Sexual assault

If this has happened to you then immediately ring the police. Do not clean any of your clothing or tidy up the area where the incident has occurred. Avoid bathing or showering, brushing your teeth, eating, drinking, smoking, consuming alcohol, taking medication, changing clothes, urinating, removing or inserting a tampon, wiping or cleaning the genital area.

You could attend a local Sexual Assault Referral Centre. The police will assist you in getting to this specialist place. You can refer yourself to such a centre.

4

PERSONAL
SAFETY

What is conflict?

Conflict is when we can into collision with someone and we have a disagreement about a particular problem. Conflict can usually be resolved by the use of respectful words and behaviour. Understanding the other person's point of view by asking questions also helps this process. Bullying and hate crime incidents at different because the abuser is consciously targeting you. The stages of conflict can go unnoticed. They start from the splitting process in the persons thinking mind and move on to name-calling, joking, negative conversation, accidental bumps, quarrels and then move onto violence.

If left untreated, minor incidents can develop into violent confrontation. It is always better to avoid confrontation in the first place. The aim of this chapter of provide you with a safety plan, that you can use in your daily life.

Plan and prepare

Awareness is simply being alert to your surroundings, planning ahead and thinking about what is in front of you. You have to be prepared for confrontation. In the case of bullying incidents research has shown that the majority of incidents happen when you on your own and in a place where there is an opportunity for secrecy. In the case of hate crime research has shown that incidents usually take place near your home and a place where your particular group meets on a weekly basis.

Write down your weekly routine on a timetable, now record where you saw the abuser and what they were doing. Identify times where you can avoid the abuser.

The danger of stubbornness

One of the main obstacles to maintaining your safety is your own attitude. Adopting the attitude of 'why should I?' can put you in real danger. You may be thinking why should I change my routines because of the abusers small mindedness. The flexibility required to successfully avoid confrontation will not last forever. In the short term 'avoidance' may be an appropriate response. Objectively consider the time of day, the day's events and information on websites. Instead of avoiding the abuser at all costs and developing a certain sense of 'paranoia', use the technique of 'avoidance' in the right circumstances.

What are the right circumstances?

❏ Avoid late-nights, and avoid peak times when people are drunk, typically on weekends between 9 PM and 2 AM. Abusive people are more dangerous when under the influence of drink or drugs.

❏ Identify where the abuser usually congregates with friends.

❑   Has something happened within the community? Are people feeling upset and angry about issues within the press or UK media?

❑   What has happened today? Has the abusers team team lost a vital match?

❑   Use the Internet to your advantage. The abuser may divulge information about his/her whereabouts and state of mind whilst using social networking sites. This information may give you a 'feel' for the likelihood of confrontation. Confrontation usually takes place when people are 'motivationally aroused'. Excitement and controversy at the biological level are factors that can determine an emotionally charged person. When viewing social networking information ask yourself one question. How is he/she feeling?

❑   Keep to main roads and avoid places of darkness. Travel along well lit and busy areas. Plan your route and consider areas where there is CCTV.

Be cautious

The abuser holds an exaggerated sense of self importance. The abuser holds the belief 'I am entitled to punish others, because I am superior'. The splitting process occurs within milliseconds. The thinking process of splitting works on many different levels. The interpretation of what the bully perceives rests on the bodily senses. What the bully sees, feels, smells, hears and experiences determines the level of judgment.

The difficulty with this process is that of assumption. As the victim of an assault or hate crime incident, you are unaware of the real reason why you are being targeted. Being in possession of the true facts that lead to the bullies splitting process is of immense importance. If you can work out how the abuser reacts in certain circumstances, you can effectively plan to manage the abusers predictable behavior patterns.

Compare and contrast a time when you were in the presence of the abuser. Makes notes about the time when you were bullied and the time when you were left alone. Ask the following questions: What was I wearing? What was I doing? Who was I with? Where was I? What was the bully doing? Was my body language defensive? Who was the bully with? What time of day? What did I say? What do I talk about? How did the bully seem? Are there any obvious signs to the bullies splitting process?

Remember 'splitting' and 'punishment' are keyword words.

What you do, what you say, how you react will have a major impact on what happens next. Whilst the abuser is 'splitting' his inner experience, inner tension is building within him. Depending on the conditioning of the abuser, what you say and how you say it may accelerate the splitting process. Whilst the splitting process accelerates the emotional tension that the abuser feels connects with the idea of 'punishment'. In order to manage a hostile situation, we need to be aware of how to reduce the emotional splitting process.

Retaliation

Any form of retaliation is problematic for a number of reasons. The abuser is judging you on a number of levels. When you retaliate with words, humor, physical confrontation or even empty threats. The abuser interprets these actions as 'bad'. The concept of 'bad' pairs with an intense feeling of anxiety. If you continue to retaliate the abuser continues to feel further anxiety. The feeling of anxiety will pave the way for the abuser to consider punishing you.

There are always three considerations that are likely to predict the outcome of being punished by an abuser. It is important to remember that this is not an exact science. Reducing and managing the splitting process is your first step to reducing the probability of being targeted.

Your response 'Target'

You are most probably feeling nervous and tense when in the presence of the abuser. Take some of the deep breaths and try to infuse some calm into your body. Remind yourself that reacting to whatever the abuser says, will in effect cause the abuser to react immediately. Say very little, and avoid retaliatory words or behavior. Try and figure out what makes the abuser tick. Use whatever means are at your disposal, consider being the 'grey man'. Try not to stand out and draw attention to yourself, when in the presence of the abuser.

Try to be in the presence of a *'capable guardian'* this includes family members, friends, and co-workers.

The location 'Place'

Places where there are an abundance of people and natural surveillance are locations where bullying is less likely to occur. Locations where there are CCTV cameras and strong community links are going to be less tolerant of abusive behavior.

Try to be in a place that has a designee who has some responsibility for controlling behavior in the specific location such as a bus driver or teacher in a school, bar owners in drinking establishments, landlords in rental housing etc.

The abuser 'Offender'

What time of day is it? Is Has the abuser taken any illegal substances or drank any alcohol? Does the abuser have any particular habits that are obvious? When is he or she likely to be more agitated?

Bystanders

Bystanders are people who are present when observing the bullying incident. Without saying or doing anything, bystanders can have a positive or a negative effect on the outcome of the bullying incident. The abuser may enjoy the feeling of power that the bystander provides. Negative bystanders may play a part in the bullies motivation. For example, negative bystanders may shout or excuse the abuser for his or her behavior. Groups of like-minded people who are part of the abusers social group may add to your problem. Positive bystanders are people who may intervene. You cannot predict the likelihood of intervention and so it would be better to avoid places where the abuser and his/her accomplices gather.
For the offender, the handler, someone who knows the offender well and who is in a position to exert some control over his or her actions. Handlers include parents, siblings, teachers, friends and spouses.

Thinking about everyday personal safety - walking the street

- ❑ Try and vary your times and locations when travelling. Do not update your Facebook location whilst on the move.

- ❑ Walk tall, look around you and focus your attention on the here and now. Tune into your surroundings and avoid thinking about what you need to be doing and what you should be doing.

- ❑ Walk with a friend and tell someone who you trust, where you're going.

- ❑ You might like to spread your valuables around your body. For example your phone in your bag, your house keys in your trouser pocket and your money in your jacket.

- ❑ Look behind you discreetly. Try and use the mirrors of cars and the reflections of shop windows.

- When walking, avoid the use of your mobile phone or texting on the go. This distraction can stop you from being alert to your surroundings.

- If you're in company with somebody and you need to answer the phone place your back to a wall and ask your friend to look left and right.

- Consider wearing sunglasses in the daytime, wraparound sunglasses can help you avoid eye contact and allow you to discreetly observe the situation.

- Be extra careful when using cashpoint machines. Make sure nobody is hovering nearby and do not count your money in the middle of the street.

- Beware of someone who warns you of the danger of walking alone and then offers to accompany you. This is a ploy some attackers have been known to use.

- Consider carrying a personal safety alarm, which can be used to shock and disorientate an attacker giving you vital seconds to get away.

- When approaching a public house, step across the road and avoid smokers and drinkers loitering outside.

- Avoid dark gloomy places, subways, bridges, open fields and dark lanes. Never take a short cut.

- Depending on the social occasion, consider what type of clothing could be a hindrance. Avoid poorer footwear, you can't run with flip-flops or high heels. Avoid wearing foodies and large anoraks, as they may block your peripheral vision and can easily be used to stop you seeing. Jewellery can be used to strangle and expensive earrings can easily be ripped out of your skin and can cause injury. Long here can be used as a tool to grapple with, so tied up. Keep expensive personal items to a minimum. When carrying a rucksack, carry it on one shoulder, if you sense there may be trouble, throw it on the floor and run.

- Place a small amount of money in the bottom of your shoe and a list of telephone numbers. You may need this money if you have to leave an area in a short amount of time.

Public transport

- Public transport can be a daunting experience and has its dangers. Plan well ahead and ask yourself whether you really need to travel. When you enter the carriage of a bus, tube or train have a good look around. Can you smell alcohol? Does anyone grab your attention? Try and position yourself near to the bus conductor or operator. If someone makes you uncomfortable and you sense trouble, get off at the next stop and re-plan your journey.

- Try to sit with other people and avoid empty carriages.

Taxis

- Get to know your local driver, and take his or her personal mobile number, that way you can ring them if you need help.

- You should always ensure that you travel in a licensed taxi by checking the vehicles signage or plate and the drivers badge. You should never agree to travel in an unlicensed vehicle with an unlicensed driver.

- When you get to your destination ask the driver to wait until you are inside.

Driving

- Park your car in well lit or busy areas, and if you park during the day think about what the area will feel like after dark.

- Lock the cars doors when you get into the vehicle.

- Use your electronic key fob in the correct way. Pressing the key once will only open the driver's door.

- Do not give lifts or accept lifts from people you do not know.

Home security

External doors

Does your front door have a robust deadlock i.e. a lock that requires a key to move the bolt forward into the frame?

You should consider upgrading your locks. If you have a wooden door more than 44mm thick, a 5-lever mortice lock is best. If you have a PVC-u door, a 3 multi-point lock is the best option.

Are your doors or frames free from damage caused by weathering or neglect? Are your front and back doors sufficiently strong to resist forced entry?

Even if you have good locks, it won't do any good if your doors and frames are not strong. You don't necessarily need to replace your doors and frames as there are products available to reinforce your doors.

However, if your doors or frames are in very poor condition you may need to replace them. If so make sure that the doorset is certificated to British Standard PAS 24.

Do you have a robust deadlock on your back door?

You should consider upgrading your locks. The locks on your back door should be the same standard as on your front door.

Do you lock your doors when you leave the house for even a few minutes?

Make sure that you always remember to lock up properly when you leave your home - even if you just pop out for a few minutes.

Do you lock your doors at all times when you're home?

Make sure you keep your doors and windows locked when you're at home, including when you're out in the garden.

Are your windows and frames in good condition?

Look at the condition of your window frames, as they can be easy to force if weakened by age. Again there are products available to reinforce them, and any new windows should be certificated to British Standard BS 7950.

Do your accessible windows (except those designated as a fire escape route) have locks with keys?

Fit locks on all your accessible windows – including those that could be reached by a nimble burglar. There are a number of good locks available which are relatively cheap and easy to fit. PVC-u windows may require specialist locks.

Do you keep your windows locked whenever you leave the house?

Make sure that you always remember to lock windows as well as your doors when you leave your home.

If you live in a flat with a communal entry, do you make sure you never buzz strangers in? When entering through communal doors, do you ensure strangers can't follow you in?

Be extra careful about letting people in through shared front doors – if you don't know them the simple advice is don't let them in.

Do you have strong locks on your shed or garage?

Set about putting a strong padlock on your garage or shed. These often hold tools which are expensive to replace and could be used to break into your house.

If your garage is attached to your house, do you have deadlocks on connecting doors?

Any door connecting your garage to your house should be treated in the same way as an external door – someone could get into the garage and work on the connecting door without being seen.

Neighbourhood watch

Are you a member of Neighbourhood Watch / Home Watch?

Consider joining such a scheme – or even starting one if there isn't one in your area. Your local community needs your help in preventing and tackling crimes like burglary. Your local Neighbourhood Police Team will be able to provide details of your local scheme.

Do you have a working burglar alarm?

Consider improving your security with a burglar alarm. Many burglars will avoid breaking into a property with an alarm and will seek out easier properties.

Do you set it whenever you leave, and at night when you go to bed?

Make sure that you always set your alarm when you leave your home and when you go to bed at night.

Are you careful not to leave keys near a door or window?

Leaving keys within reach of a window, glass pane or in a lock could make a thief's job easier.

Do you make sure you don't have spare keys hidden outside?

It is not a good idea to leave keys outside. Burglars know that people hide spare keys under flowerpots, under doormats or in garages.

Do you ask friends to remove your post, turn on lights and open your curtains?

Take a few steps when going away on holiday to appear as though you are really at home. Ask a friend to open or shut curtains, turn lights on and off and remove your post. Cancel delivery of milk and papers.

Do you leave a light on, other than the hall light, and shut the curtains?

Consider installing automatic switches to turn lights on whilst you are out in the evening and remember to shut the curtains.

Do you make use of the door spy hole and security chain when you have a visitor?
Do you check IDs of strangers who say they are from a utility company?

Take extra precautions when answering the door if you're not expecting visitors; use a spy hole or security chain, and check IDs carefully if visitors say they're from utility companies or the council.

There are a number of lone worker systems, that may improve your access to safety. Lone worker systems use GPS tracking technology, voice recording technology and direct contact to emergency services. The use of the systems may enhance the safety of hate crime victims. The Suzy Lamplugh Trust has devised a guide to Lone worker systems and it is available from their website.

What happens to us when we are confronted with violence?

When we are confronted with the threat of violence we can become scared or angry. You will notice many swirling feelings within your body. You may feel extremely nervous with butterflies in your stomach. Some people feel sick and paralysed with fear. All these feelings are perfectly normal. This is an aspect of fear called the fight or flight response. Evolution has prepared you for the threat of violence. Your prehistoric brain has developed a natural response to the threat of violence. Thousands of years ago our ancestors relied on this response daily. Our ancestors had to avoid predators and fight with warring tribes. Your body is preparing to run or fight.

Unfortunately the threat of violence is still with us today, however, it is small when we compare it to what our ancestors had to go through. Our brain transmits messages to the adrenal glands. These special glands release adrenaline. The hormone adrenaline is a special transmitter and travels around the body in an instant. It makes your heart beat quicker, your breathing rate increases, you become stronger and your tolerance to pain increases. Your reactions become faster and you can run and jump further. You are ready for action.

Sometimes when our abuser torments us this natural reaction can have the reverse effect. You may become more agitated and stressed. Sometimes this can make the situation worse. If you feel yourself getting uptight and nervous take some deep breaths and say to yourself, "It is normal to feel like this". You will remain calmer. Fear is only natural, as such try and control your fear and remain receptive to the events unfolding in front of you.

What is happening to the abuser prior to becoming violent?

The abuser at this point is going through a period of intense anger. The abuser loses all mental control. The abuser's mind is making the situation worse, repeating and re-living all the anger and frustration. However, if you remain calm in a confrontational situation you are in control. Being able to think is the key to diffusing conflict and avoiding violence.

Situational awareness

Ask the following questions: keep your head up and look around you. Every now and again look behind you. Gather information and use your eyes and ears. Has the abuser been drinking? How many people are there? Who could possibly help?

The stare

The abuser will hold a stare across the room, and is looking for you to catch his/her gaze. This stage of awareness is an opportunity for you to avoid confrontation. Do not make it obvious but keep a watch over the abuser.

The question and approach

If you have been indecisive and have not avoided the abuser, you are ready for the next stage of confrontation. Your abuser is going to project feelings of inadequacy onto you and make you the problem. They will say, "Have you got a problem with me?". What they are really saying is, "I am insecure, and I have a problem with you". Be aware that at this stage the abuser has already planned to attack you. The abuser may attack you verbally or physically, depending on the circumstances.

The body language

Body language will change as the situation escalates. Even at the first stage look for the vital signs of body language that demonstrates violence. Communication is mostly through body language. They will get closer to you. The following description is equally applicable to men and women. Your abuser's chest will be inflated like a balloon, and arms will puff outwards like a bird. They will stand tall and appear robotic. When talking they will use hands and point in a stabbing motion. The face will redden, eyes will bulge, and teeth may show. The jaw will tighten and they will appear bigger. The abuser will constantly look around and may stamp the floor.

The provocation

Here it becomes increasingly tense. The abuser will mutter words like, "Yeah, yeah, so, so". At this stage it will be almost impossible to communicate with them. What the abuser is doing is target picking. The provocation can last some time depending on the abuser. A violent abuser will build up to this stage in a matter of split seconds. They will also swear at you.

The Attack

The distance between you and the abuser will shorten and they may look for an opportunity to attack. This will depend your own body language. The majority of attackers are right-handed and right-footed. Do you know if your abuser is right or left-handed? In most cases your abuser is going to throw a right-hand hooking punch to the head. This isn't always the case as some like to grab and pull your hair.

What Can I Do About It?

You cannot change an abuser, only an abuser can do that. You have to adapt to the abuser's behaviour and make quick decisions.

Situational Awareness

Keep your head up and look around you, and every now and again look behind you.

Gather information, and use your eyes and ears. Anticipate problems before they arise. Think Safety **PLAN**.

The stare and approach

It is absolutely normal to avoid confrontation and aggression - avoid the abuser and leave the area. There are many factors to consider at this stage. Is he or she bigger and more aggressive than you? Has he or she been drinking alcohol? Does they have a history of violence? Prepare yourself if your sixth sense starts to answer "yes" to these questions. Do you have a panic alarm handy? Where are you going to run?

Consider trickery

The abuser may try and entice you into what is called a deceptive attack. What they will do is ask a stupid question and then attack you. (This is a technique that distracts and confuses you).

The question *"HAVE YOU GOT A PROBLEM WITH ME?"*

If your bully comes close then step away, keep your hands up, and turn your palms outwards. Stand at a 45 degree angle. Tuck your chin in and talk at a distance. Move side to side when talking to them. Say to them firmly; *"NO, I DON'T WANT TROUBLE. I DON'T WANT TO FIGHT."* Don't turn your back on them and keep to the wall. Appear to give in to them. Remember that by complying with their rules you are giving them a sense of control. You are also playing for time and preparing to respond.

The body language

Appear non-confrontational and keep your hands and palms facing outwards. This is a ploy as it tells the abuser you are not willing to fight and gives them a sense of power. Tell them what they want to hear and keep on saying it even if it is, "I am sorry, I am sorry". Give them power.

The provocation

Do not argue and try to remain calm. Keep well away from them. They are dangerous but you have options: you can run away, you can activate your panic alarm or you can defend yourself.

The attack

If you are getting attacked keep moving away from them. Cover your face and try and protect yourself. Do not let them get too close. Keep on shouting, "HELP, HELP'

The hate crime perspective

All the personal safety advice in this chapter assumes capability. However in the case of hate crime victim's capability is the sole reason why victims are being targeted in the first place.

A wheelchair user can't effectively get away from a group of tormenting abusers. However a lone workers system could summons help immediately. A deaf person has to move forward in order to hear somebody's voice.

Mate Crime is the exploitation, abuse or theft from people with a Learning Disability, by those they consider as their friends. To learn about mate crime visit the website www.arcsafety.net

A persons religious and cultural traditions bond that person to a certain type of dress and routine. These factors may reduce the opportunities for personal safety. If you do have concerns about your safety, consider speaking to the spiritual advisor of your particular religion and seek clarification. Depending on your particular needs consider writing your own safety plan and factor in your own particular issues of capability.

Meetings

If you chose use the internet or personal ads to meet for people for socialising it's worth having a few basic safety strategies.

People can lie! People may not be who they say they are, and you won't know for sure until you meet them. Chat as much as you can to someone before meeting – find out as much as you can. If they are reluctant to give any info, think carefully about them.

Meet in public: if you meet them, insist in meeting in a bar, café, or somewhere public. Then you can check them out for real. Avoid inviting them round or going to their home before meeting them first, even for a short while, so you can trust your instincts better.

Tell someone: not always possible, we know, especially if you're not out, but try to leave some indication of where you are going with someone you trust.

5

THE INTERNET
AND CYBER-
BULLYING

Imagine throwing a pebble into a pond. As the pebble immerses itself with the water surface, the energy contained within the pebble causes the water particles to form a small set of waves. The waves ripple out in all directions. No matter what objects there are in the pond, the waves make contact with those objects.

The Internet is just like the pond, the energy of our thoughts, emotions and our intentions are just like the pebbles that we throw. The waves that we create, curl and crash into all directions. The objects that stand in their way are not stationary but can direct their thoughts and emotions towards us. This creates conflict, and it is it this conflict that could make matters worse. The audience that you are connected to, are connected to larger audiences. Every word, sound and video can be copied and past too others. Whenever somebody views your profile, try to consider the splitting process. Ask the following questions. Is my profile going to infuriate the people who hold certain opinions about me? How can I adapt my profile in order to reduce the chances of being targeted? The perception that others hold about you is just as important as it is within a cyber-world. The Internet creates a sense of pseudo safety. From the comfort of our own homes we can express who we really are from a computer. The expressions of our inner selves allows us to feel a certain amount of contentment. However this expression can become costly, because in the world of bullying and hate crime, we are giving the abuser intimate information about our real thoughts and feelings. Our innermost secrets are only ours and for sharing with our trusted friends.

Mobile Phones

It's a good idea to only give your number out to friends who you know in the real world. If your mobile number is given to people that you don't know, they may hassle you. This is why it's also best not to put your number on your profile of your social networking site (like Bebo, MySpace and Facebook).

Whilst having a camera phone is cool and really useful, be careful if you share your photos with others. Pictures can be changed or shared around, so think about what the image is and who you are sending it to, before you press send. Once it's out there it's out there forever!

Bluetoothing is a quick and easy way of sharing stuff like photos, files and music. It's important to be aware that unless you lock your Bluetooth, anyone in the area can access things in your phone, like your contacts. If you don't want to share this information with strangers (why would you?!), then make sure you lock your Bluetooth.

It's also a good idea to change your password from the default setting of 0000 so people can't guess it. Locking your Bluetooth can help reduce the risk of getting viruses or spam to your mobile

The worrying thing about the social networking using GPS technology, is that your contacts will be on a map, showing exactly where they are. If you can see them, your contacts can also see where you are too. Quite scary if you have contacts on your profile that you don't know or don't trust. If you do want to use these sort of apps, you need to remember to use your privacy settings and remove anyone you don't know or don't trust, from your contacts.

Social Networking

Be careful what information you give out on your profile. Remember that you don't know who your friend's friends are… or your friend's friends' friends! And you don't know what they'll do with your picture or your phone number if you give it out by mistake. Once your picture is out there, it's out there forever and you won't be able to get it back.

Be aware that information on your profile could potentially be viewed by anyone. So if you wouldn't be comfortable printing it off and handing it out on the street, maybe it shouldn't be on your profile.

Smoke and mirrors

Use a nickname or your initials instead of your name – you don't want just anyone knowing who you are. Consider changing your photo to a cool graphic or picture of your favourite band, that way strangers won't have access to a picture of you. It's not a great idea to post where you're going on your profile or twitter or where you live. Think through if you'd want everyone who can view the post to turn up at any time!

Who to chat to...

Think through who you want to chat to and how many of your personal thoughts you want anyone to view. Sometimes, it can seem a good idea to share what you got up to with your boyfriend last night, or the argument you had with your best mate; but as you're writing – remember that information could be public forever! It is tempting to share loads of stuff on your profile, especially since you're often typing from the comfort of your own home. But remember, the internet is a public space. Be careful who you agree to accept into your forums / private chat areas. If you know someone… who knows someone… who knows someone, it doesn't make them your friend, so think carefully about whether you should be chatting to them and what kind of things you're saying.

Use your Privacy Settings. Adjust your account settings (sometimes called "Privacy Settings") so only approved friends can instant message you. This won't ruin your social life – new people can still send you friend requests and message you, they just won't be able to pester you via IM. This means that people you don't want to see your profile can't!

Some social networking sites are really well run and the administrators will try to help you remember to keep your personal information to yourself. Others are not so good – so be careful when choosing which areas you go to.

Don't post your phone number or email address on your homepage. Think about it – why would anyone actually need this info when they can message you privately via your social networking site?

Tick the "no pic forwarding" option on your settings page – this will stop people forwarding your pictures to anyone without your consent.

Don't give too much away in a blog. Yes, tell the world you're going to a party on Saturday night. But don't post details of where it is. Real friends can phone you to get details, why would a complete stranger need to know this information?

Save all evidence you have of the bullying. If you have nasty emails or things posted on your profile save them to your machine so you can use it as proof. Save texts or voicemails that say anything horrible. Learn how to **block the bully** on IM or delete them from your contacts.

Try not to reply or retaliate to things they say or do; it might make the situation worse. If you don't respond, they are more likely to get bored and move on.

If you are being bothered via text, contact your service provider. Each network has a special area for this sort of problem. Check out their website or call them for advice or a free number change.

Contacts:

- ❑ **O2**: ncb@o2.com or 08705214000
- ❑ **Vodafone**: 191 from a Vodafone phone or 08700700191 (pay monthly) & 08700776655 (pay as you go)
- ❑ **3**: call 333 from a 3 phone or 0870733033
- ❑ **Orange**: Call 450 on an Orange phone or 07973100450
- ❑ **T-Mobile**: Call 150 on a T-mobile phone or 08454125000

Although bullying is not a specific criminal offence in UK law, criminal and civil laws can apply in terms of, for example, harassment or threatening behaviour, and particularly relevant for cyberbullying – threatening and menacing communications:

- ❑ Protection from Harassment Act 1997, which has both criminal and civil provision
- ❑ Malicious Communications Act 1988
- ❑ Section 43 of the Telecommunications Act 1984
- ❑ Communications Act 2003
- ❑ Public Order Act 1986

6

LAW AND THE CRIMINAL JUSTICE SYSTEM

The police

The police are a key 24 hour agency for people who are experiencing bullying and hate crime. They should be the first people you call for in an emergency. The police have a number of short to long term practical solutions that can help your distressing set of circumstances.

If you call 999 the police will attend as quickly as possible and can offer the following interventions:

Short term – They can arrest and take away the abuser using a number of police powers. This ensures that you are safe from harm and that you get some time to relax and consider your needs and options available to you. The police may arrange for first aid or medical treatment.

Medium term – The police will ask you a number of questions and will risk assess your current living arrangements. This will ensure that a care plan is followed up and other agencies are aware of the victimisation that you are experiencing. You may be referred to other agencies who can support you. For example victim support, housing, counselling etc.

The police can be used to intervene and formally warn people by the use of the harassment act 1997 (covered in detail). Sometimes bullying incidents only require an intervention such as this. The police also have new powers with respect to alcohol related disorder. They can order an abuser to leave a particular area and not return for a period of twenty four hours. Some police officers are also trained in a process known as 'restorative justice'. Restorative justice has been tested and shown to work in solving street bullying issues and it may be an option offered to you. Restorative justice approaches are not used in stalking, relationship and hate crime incidents.

Every police service in the UK takes hate crime very seriously. Every police officer has received training in hate crime and each local policing district has a specially appointed 'hate crime officer'. This officer is the link between you and all the agencies that can support you. Ask to speak to your local hate crime officer.

Long term – The police can help, support and investigate an allegation of wrong doing. For example if you have been assaulted, harassed or your property has been damaged. The police are the first agency within the criminal justice system and will guide you from reporting a crime to the actual conviction of the abuser. The role of the police is to investigate crime and secure the necessary evidence. The police can also advise you with regard to your personal safety. A crime prevention officer can be called upon to install panic alarms and secure your home correctly. If you are concerned about your personal safety and would like to be referred to a crime prevention officer please ask this to be recorded on the police risk assessment form. NB service standards vary across the UK.

The legal system explained simply

The Legal System can be compared to making a special film. The writers of the film's script are lawyers and judges. They decide what script will be used, and they write the law. You are an actor in the film, but you can alter the film's story. You have been involved in an incident and you contact the police. The police act as the film makers, and have a film crew, director and many assistants. They record what you have to say, they organise make-up artists and runners. The police take photos of what has happened. They contact other actors and record what they have got to say. They also interview the person who has abused you and record what he or she has got to say. The police make your film and present it to a Crown Prosecution Service (CPS) solicitor. The CPS are known as the DPP in Scotland. The CPS solicitor edits the film and will decide if the film is of a good standard. The CPS decides whether the film can be released to the general public and then release it to the courts. The CPS, not the police, decides to prosecute the abuser. The courts receive the film and the person abusing you has an opportunity to say if the film was recorded correctly and that they have been abusing you. If the person abusing you decides not to admit that the film was correctly made he/she can then ask the court to play the making of the film. The court watches the making of the film and then decides if the person abusing you has acted against the law. The judge or magistrate in the court then punishes the abuser for breaking the law.

Criminal Law

The criminal law is used by many different agencies not just the police. This type of law is administered in a Magistrate's Court and Crown Court. Less serious offences are dealt with in the Magistrate's Court. The legal system requires a hefty weight of evidence and a case has to be proved beyond reasonable doubt.

UK law

In England and Wales there isn't a law that protects you against bullying and hate crime specifically. However, there are many laws that can be used depending on what has happened to you. Hate Crime is a standard term that considers gender, disability, race etc. However following a number of high profile cases the government decided to give the courts extra powers to deal with incidents of racially or religiously aggravated offences. Gender, LGBT and disability are not included within these powers.

- ❏ Common Assault
- ❏ Actual Bodily Harm
- ❏ Grievous Bodily Harm without intent

- ☐ Grievous Bodily Harm with intent

- ☐ Domestic Burglary

- ☐ Harassment

Miscellaneous Offences (Criminal Law)

- ☐ Blackmail

- ☐ Kidnap

- ☐ Racially aggravated offences

- ☐ Using violence to secure entry into premises

- ☐ Sexual offences

- ☐ Public order offences

In England and Wales the legislation is covered in:

Section 28 of the Crime and Disorder Act 1998 provides a definition of the term 'racially or religiously aggravated' for the purposes of section 29 (aggravated assaults), section 30 (aggravated criminal damage), section 31 (aggravated public order) and section 32 (aggravated harassment).

28(1) An offence is racially or religiously aggravated for the purposes of sections 29 to 32 if-

(a) at the time of committing the offence, or immediately before or after doing so, the offender demonstrates towards the victim of the offence hostility based on the victim's membership (or presumed membership) of a racial or religious group; or

(b) the offence is motivated (wholly or partly) by hostility towards members of a racial or religious group based on their membership of that group.

28(2) In subsection (1)(a)-

membership,

in relation to a racial or religious group, includes association with members of that group;

presumed

means presumed by the offender.

28(3) It is immaterial for the purposes of paragraph (a) or (b) of subsection (1) whether or not the offender's hostility is also based, to any extent, on any other factor not mentioned in that paragraph.

28(4) In this section **Racial Group** means a group of persons defined by reference to race, colour, nationality (including citizenship) or ethnic or national origins.

In Scotland the law is different

The new law is called the Offences (Aggravation by Prejudice) (Scotland) Act. It will mean that homo/biphobic, transphobic and disability-prejudice crime is properly recognised as hate crime.

This is the first transgender-inclusive hate crime legislation in Europe, and has the most inclusive definition of transgender identity in any European legislation.

From tomorrow, any criminal offence which is partly or wholly motivated by prejudice on grounds of disability, sexual orientation or transgender identity, will be dealt with as a hate crime all the way through the system.

The offence could for example be an assault, or vandalism, or verbal threats and abuse which can be charged as breach of the peace, or any other crime. If the person committing the offence uses homo/biphobic, transphobic, or disability-prejudice language, or if there is any other evidence of their prejudiced motive, that makes it a hate crime.

If anyone witnessing a crime thinks it was a hate crime, the police must record it as a hate incident. If there is any evidence of the hate motive, for example prejudiced language was used, it will be charged as a hate crime. If the person charged is found guilty, the hate motive will be taken into account in sentencing - and the court must say publicly what difference the hate motive made to the sentence.

Community Legal Advice

Community Legal Advice is a free and confidential advice service paid for by legal aid. We can advise you via a national telephone helpline, website, advice centers and digital TV. Helpline number *0845 345 4 345 www.communitylegaladvice.org.uk*

Focussing on the Harassment Act 1997

The protection from harassment act 1997 introduced measures for protection under both the criminal and civil law, and also provides a link between criminal and civil law. The provisions include to criminal offences; the offence of criminal harassment (under S.2 a summary offence, tried in the magistrates court) and a more serious offence involving fear of violence (under S.4 triable either as a summary offence, or as an indictable offence in the Crown Court). If convicted of either of these offences, there is an additional measure for protection: a restraining order can also be granted by the court, stopping the offender from further similar conduct.

Under S.2 (the offence of criminal harassment) a person must not pursue a course of conduct which amounts to harassment of another, and which he knows, or ought to know, amounts to harassment of the other, ie if any 'reasonable person' is in possession of the same information would regard such conduct as harassment. The term 'reasonable person' may be problematic in practice, but the aim of the legislation is to shift the emphasis from a subjective harmful intent of the abuser, which is often difficult to prove, to what actually happens and its effects on the victim.

A course of conduct includes: sending abusive text messages, stalking, sending letters, cyber bullying, verbal threats and graffiti. Your bullying diary explains how to collect the evidence for this offence.

Under s.4 (the offence involving fear of violence) anyone who's course of conduct causes another to fear, on at least two occasions, that violence would be used against them is guilty of an offence. The abuser has to know or ought to know that his course of conduct will have caused the other to fear that violence was going to be used against them. A course of conduct, that causes someone to be in fear of violence, can be difficult to prove. The chapter relating to personal safety and confrontation may help you describe the threatening incident in more detail. The police can arrest without warrant anyone who they suspect of committing either of these offences under separate incidents do not have to be the same time each time. For example, cyber bullying on Monday, followed by verbally abuse on Tuesday and graffiti on Wednesday will constitute related course of conduct.

Practically speaking the police use a formal first warning procedure in most cases. If this is offered to you, record the name of the officer, the date you made the written statement at the incident number. Record these details in your bullying diary.

Making the first call to the police

When the police arrive, tell the police officers what has exactly happened and how you feel. Explain to them the types of abuse that you have been exposed to. Tell the police that you want to be safe and want the abuser to be taken away. Answer all questions as honestly as possible. It may make the difference to the type of risk assessment that is carried out.

The police officers who have attended may ask you the following questions:

- ❑   Do you want to make a complaint against the abuser?

- ❑   Do you want to press charges against the abuser?

- ❑   Are you willing to attend court?

These types of questions are not supportive and do not explain clearly the on-going support and care that you will receive. The word complaint is misunderstood. By making a **statement** you are asking the police officer to listen and record what type of mistreatment you have suffered. You are asking the officer to seize and preserve evidence of a crime. You are asking the officer to be supportive from the very beginning, allowing the officer to liaise with other specialists who can and will support you. And lastly you are asking the officer to support you in the event of a court case. Not all cases get to court. Making a statement to the police ensures that you are guided along the paths of people who understand you and wish to help you. It is not as daunting as you will first think.

Making a statement to the police

The police will ask you a number of questions and draft a rough statement. They will then clarify and delve deeper into what has happened. It is at this stage a statement will be written. It is important to understand that it is your statement and it should be written in your own language.

You may have to be video interviewed. This is a procedure that provides the police with the best possible evidence. This evidence can be played to the Court. Tell the police exactly what happened, including what you saw and heard. Tell them if you fear for your, or your family's safety. Tell them if the crime was made worse by abuse related to race, sexuality, religion or disability. Whilst at your home the police may take photographs, arrange an appointment with your GP or even take you to hospital. After the evidential statement has been taken, you will be asked to provide a Victim Personal Statement.

Making a victim personal statement

A Victim Personal Statement (VPS) is a written account of how you feel and how the abuse has affected you. The VPS will be used after the abuser has been convicted in a court of law. After a traumatic event has taken place it can be very difficult to put into words how the trauma has affected you. It may be some time before you can clearly express yourself. Don't worry, you can add to your statement at a later time.

Here are some guidelines that you might like to think about:

- ❏ How has the crime affected your life?

- ❏ Bail – Do you have any concerns about the suspect being bailed?

- ❏ Information – How often would you like to be updated?

- ❏ Concerns – What concerns do you have about the court process?

- ❏ Are you going to claim compensation?

- ❏ Would you like the police to apply for a Restraining Order if your abuser is convicted at court?

- ❏ Has your behaviour changed because you have been abused?

- ❏ Socialising – Do you see friends and relatives less?

- ❏ Self Esteem – Do you feel trapped and less confident?

- ❏ Heath- Are you sleeping at night? Are you suffering on going health issues?

- ❏ Future - Are you nervous about the future?

- ❏ Feelings – Are you suffering from panic attacks or anxiety?

❏ Restraining Order - If you are still concerned about your personal safety ask the police to apply for a restraining order on conviction.

Special measures

The witness service and police will support you. If you are a vulnerable witness the police will assess this prior or during your interview statement. What this means is that the police and CPS will be able to apply to the court for special measures. Special measures are instructions that allow the court to become more people friendly.

For instance a victim can request the following:

❏ Physically placing a screening between the witness and the abuser in Crown Court.

❏ Evidence from the witness by live link (via a video camera) in Crown Court and Magistrates' Courts. You won't have to enter court and you won't see your abuser.

❏ Evidence given in private in Crown Court and Magistrates' Courts.

❏ Removal of wigs and gowns in court (not applicable for magistrates).

❏ The use of video recorded evidence in court paints a true picture.

How do I strengthen my case?

In order for you to be successful in court you have to give as much detail as you possibly can, and don't leave anything out. If you have been dishonest tell the police in the first instance. If you omit something from your statement you will undermine your case. Be honest. Never take matters into your own hands, as you will weaken your case and jeopardise your chances of a successful outcome.

What should I do after I have given a statement?

After you have given your statement, it may be a good time to speak to a person who understands your experiences, supports your needs and can arrange further support. It's only a phone call - please make that call. You are not alone.

What is an arrest?

An arrest is the use of a legal power to force the abuser to be detained at a designated police station. The reasoning for an arrest may be due to a number of factors, these include:

Preventing serious further harm being caused; investigating an allegation of a crime or preventing further crimes being committed against you.

What happens to the abuser at the police station?

The abuser will be well treated and looked after. Firstly a risk assessment will be carried out ensuring that the police understand the abuser's needs. If the abuser requires medical treatment or medication then these needs will be met. The abuser will be given an opportunity to sober up from either the influence of alcohol or drugs. The abuser has the following rights:

❑ The right to speak to a duty solicitor.

❑ The right to inform someone that they are being detained at the police station. They will not contact you.

❑ The right to read the codes of practice detailing the way in which the police should treat them.

❑ Once the officer in the case (OIC) has thoroughly investigated the circumstances of the crime he or she will then interview the abuser. This will give the abuser an opportunity to give their side of the story.

❑ The police have strictly limited powers as to the length of time they can keep an abuser at the police station (usually 24 hours) and they cannot impose conditions when forced to release him or her on police bail.

What do the police do after arrest?

After the police have gathered all available evidence and interviewed the abuser the case is then passed to the Crown Prosecution Service (CPS). The CPS decides whether there is enough evidence for a criminal conviction. The CPS applies a number of tests and considers if the matter needs to be resolved in a court of law. If the CPS decides that your case merits action by the courts they will direct the police to charge the person.

In Scotland

If the police think there is enough information to take a case to court, they will report the case to the Procurator Fiscal. Once a case has gone to the Fiscal it is no longer the responsibility of the police: all they can tell you is that they have sent it to the Fiscal and ask you to contact the Fiscal's office for further information. The Procurator Fiscal will decide whether to prosecute the person accused of the crime. If you want to get in touch with your local Fiscal, call: 0131 226 2626 to get their details or look them up on **www.copfs.gov.uk**. If the crime was committed by someone under 18, the case may have been referred to the Scottish Children's Reporter (SCRA) and may be dealt with at a Children's Hearing. Victims and witnesses do not attend a Children's Hearing, as confidential information about the child's family will be discussed. You can find out more at **www.scra.gov.uk** If you are needed to give evidence in court as a witness for the prosecution, you will be sent a letter from the Procurator Fiscal. If you are unable to attend court, you must inform the Fiscal immediately. If you have a concern about your personal privacy, you should inform the Fiscal as early as possible. Court hearings are held in public, but the Fiscal can ask the judge or sheriff who hears the case for special measures to protect your privacy. If someone is charged with the crime and you are worried about them being released on bail, you should tell the police officer you are dealing with, the Procurator Fiscal, or your solicitor about any concerns as soon as possible. You should receive information from the Victim Information and Advice service, based at the Fiscal's office, who will keep you informed about what is happening about prosecuting the case. Victim Information and Advice (VIA) can be contacted via your local Fiscal's office, or on their national number: 0844 561 3701.

What does the term "charging" mean?

Charging in simple language means that a CPS solicitor, after having independently reviewed the evidence before them, believes that the abuser's wrong doing can be realistically proved in a court of law and it is in the public's interest to prosecute the abuser for his or her wrong doing.

What is bail?

Bail is an agreed set of boundaries that the abuser agrees with the police, or court, in order to comply with the criminal justice system. The abuser understands that he or she is free to do whatever they please, however, they must surrender to the court and comply with certain conditions. The conditions that the abuser signs up to are designed to protect both the abuser and the victim. The police only have the power to impose bail conditions on an arrested person following a charge. The decision to charge someone to court means that the CPS believes that there is enough evidence to prove that the abuser has broken the law.

What type of bail conditions can I ask for?

You will be consulted; however, it is the decision of the police to ensure proportionate conditions are imposed. For example:

❑   Not to contact you either directly or indirectly.

❑   Not to enter your street or town.

❑   Not to drink alcohol.

❑   A curfew from 10 pm till 8pm.

You must tell the police how frightened you are.

What is a remand in custody?

Where the crime committed is very serious, and there is evidence that the abuser will not abide by strict bail conditions, the police can apply to hold the abuser in custody. In simple terms the abuser will be held in custody until the court's first hearing. The court will decide whether the abuser is released and given court bail or remanded in custody until the actual court case. If you haven't been updated you may want to contact the local police station or the nearest magistrates court.

First Hearing

You will be notified of the first court hearing, at this stage you do not need to attend court. This is an opportunity for your abuser to plead guilty at an early stage. If this isn't the case, you will then be notified of a trial date.

Will the abuser or the defence lawyer be given my address?

No, your address is recorded on the front of your statement. Only your statement is given to all persons involved in your case.

Who will read my statement?

Everyone involved with the case will read your statement (eg police, CPS, defence, magistrate or judge).

What if someone tries to intimidate me?

It is a criminal offence to intimidate a witness.

How will I be supported?

You will be appointed a victim care officer. This person will keep you updated about the case and will assess your individual needs. You may receive financial support with regard to childcare arrangements and travel etc. Victim support can arrange a visit to a court room; this will allow you to get a feel for the entire process. This is a worthwhile experience, as familiarity can allow you to relax and understand the entire process.

What will happen If I don't go to court?

If you have any problems or concerns about going to court, you must inform the witness care officer as soon as possible. The court in certain circumstances issue a summons, that acts as an order to attend.

Going to court

On the actual day get up nice and early and remember to practise a relaxation method before you set of on your journey. This could be as simple as remembering a positive statement or listening to music. Before you leave your home remember to take with you your bullying /hate crime abuse diary. Arrange to be supported and take a good friend. On arrival make no attempts to look at your abuser or abuser's family. Identify a court room official and ask for the "Prosecution Witness Room".

The victim support officer will check you in and you will be asked if you require your written statement. This will serve to refresh your memory. Ask your solicitor or the court usher (the person who tells you to go into the court rooms) what to call the judges.

In a Magistrate's Court it is usually Sir or Madam. In other courts it may be Your Honour or Your Lordship/Ladyship. When the judge or magistrate arrives everyone stands up. Watch for what the court people do. Sit down when they do. For a detailed explanation of the court system, please visit a video tutorial at **www.talkandsupport.co.uk/victims-of-crime.html**

Giving Evidence

You will be required to give evidence so that the court can hear what has happened to you. Two solicitors will question you regarding your statement. Firstly the prosecution solicitor will ask you a number of questions. Take your time; you don't have to rush in and answer at once. If you misunderstood the question ask the solicitor to repeat the question. Speak slowly and surely. The defence solicitor will then ask some further questions. Be prepared to be a little unsettled. Again take your time and answer slowly. None of the questioning is aimed at you personally.

Trial events

The court case will be run in chronological order, and after all witnesses have given their evidence it will be the turn of the abuser to answer a number of questions.

After all the evidence is heard the magistrate or judge will retire and decide the verdict; either the abuser is guilty or not guilty.

Conviction

Once the court has decided the outcome the abuser will not necessarily be punished on that same day. The court will ask for a number of key agencies to conduct a number of reports. These will form the basis of a pre-sentence report. It may be a number of weeks before the actual punishment or rehabilitation is considered.

What the court can do

The courts have a number of powers, they could:

- ❑ Grant a prison sentence.
- ❑ Issue a restraining order.
- ❑ Community Service and a financial penalty.
- ❑ Offer the abuser help with alcohol and drug abuse.
- ❑ Order the abuser to pay you a financial sum of money.

- ❏ Order the abuser to do unpaid work in the community.

What is the Criminal Injuries Compensation Authority?

CICA is the government body responsible for administering the Criminal Injuries Compensation Scheme in England, Scotland and Wales.
Victims of violent crime The CICA provide a free service to victims of violent crime. Telephone helpline **0800 358 3601**

Am I eligible for Criminal Injuries Compensation?

You may be eligible to apply if:

- ❏ You have been injured seriously enough to qualify for at least our minimum award (£1,000).

- ❏ You were injured in an act of violence in England, Scotland or Wales. An offender does not necessarily have to have been convicted of, or even charged with that crime.

- ❏ You have made your application within two years of the incident that caused your injury. (But we might accept applications outside this limit if in your particular case it wasn't reasonable for an application form to have been submitted within two years of the incident and there would still be enough evidence for us to consider.)

But you will not be eligible if:

- ❏ You were injured before 1 August 1964

- ❏ You have already applied for compensation for the same criminal injury, under the 2008 Scheme or under any earlier Scheme operating in England, Scotland and Wales.

- ❏ The injury happened before 1 October 1979 and you and the person who injured you were living together at the time as members of the same family in the same household.

- ❏ The injury and the act of violence took place outside England, Scotland or Wales.

Victim support plus

Victim Support is the national charity giving free and confidential help to victims of crime, witnesses, their family, friends and anyone else affected across England and Wales. They also speak out as a national voice for victims and witnesses and campaign for change. They are not a government agency or part of the police and you don't have to report a crime to the police to get their help. You can call them any time after the crime has happened, whether it was yesterday, last week or several years ago. They have offices throughout England and Wales, and run the Witness

Service in every criminal court.

Call Victim Supportline on **0845 30 30 30.**

Other legal remedies

The police are not the only agency that can use legal powers in order to protect victims of hate crime. Housing associations, local councils and the civil courts are all options available to you. It is worth contact your local office and booking an appointment.

Councils and housing association tenants

Most tenants can be evicted for antisocial behaviour in certain circumstances. The chances of this happening depend on who the landlord is and the type of tenancy.

Eviction should only be used by councils and housing associations as a last resort. They are more likely to take action against antisocial behaviour in other ways, such as by asking the court to **demote the tenancy** or applying for an **antisocial behaviour order (ASBO).**

However, if you or someone in your household is behaving antisocially, the risk of losing your home if the behaviour continues is very real. The council or housing association's action will probably depend on:

❑   the seriousness of the antisocial behaviour

❑   whether they have already tried to take action in other ways, and

❑   whether the behaviour has improved.

Councils and housing associations must have specific legal reasons ('grounds') and must follow special procedures if they want to evict a tenant. However, some council and housing association tenants can be evicted fairly easily, so you should not assume that it won't happen. You are particularly at risk if you have:

❑   an introductory council tenancy

❑   a starter tenancy with a housing association

❑   a demoted council tenancy or a demoted housing association tenancy

❑   a family intervention tenancy

❑   a temporary tenancy that was granted when you made a homelessness application.

Tenants of private landlords

Most private tenants can be evicted for causing nuisance or annoyance to neighbours, or for using the property for illegal or immoral purposes (or allow someone else to do so).

What is an antisocial behaviour order?

An antisocial behaviour order is an order, given out by a court, to stop a person from behaving in a certain way or doing certain things. It's not meant to be a punishment - the idea is to prevent the person from causing further distress and alarm.

ASBOs contain specific terms and conditions that say exactly what the person cannot do, or where they cannot go. For example, an ASBO may say that a person can't play loud music at certain times or that they can't hang about in your street. The conditions in an ASBO might only apply for a limited time or indefinitely. Not every ASBO has the same conditions - each one is for a different person and for dealing with different circumstances.

An ASBO is a civil court order. This means that it is not a criminal conviction and doesn't give a person a criminal record. However, ASBOs are not an easy way out for the person who has been causing problems. They are just a different way of tackling the issues and preventing the antisocial behaviour. If someone doesn't stick to the conditions set out in an ASBO that has been made against them, they can be prosecuted.

What is an 'ASBO on conviction'?

This is where an ASBO is made against a person as part of their sentence if they have been found guilty of a crime.

What is an 'interim ASBO'?

This is a temporary ASBO, which the courts can make until they've been able to consider all the evidence and decide what to do in the long term. A court is most likely to do this if there's any potential danger to the public, although they will consider the evidence to decide whether or not an interim order is appropriate in the circumstances.

When can ASBOs be used?

ASBOs can be used in a variety of different situations where there is ongoing antisocial behaviour. For example, ASBOs can be used when support (such as negotiation and mediation) has been tried or warnings have been given but the behaviour has not improved. ASBOs can also be used at an early stage alongside support like this. In most cases, there are other solutions that can be tried before applying for an ASBO. It's important to remember that every situation is different and may need a different approach.

ASBOs can be granted to deal with problem neighbours and other disturbances in your neighbourhood and they can be used in many different situations as long as the person who is acting antisocially and the people affected by the behaviour do not live in the same household. For example, they can be used to deal with antisocial behaviour in shopping centres or even bus or train stations.

However, ASBOs won't be appropriate in every situation. For example, if you have been arguing with your neighbours over who owns the boundary between your houses, but you neighbour hasn't actually behaved antisocially, an ASBO wouldn't be the right way to deal with the problem and the court probably wouldn't grant one.

What happens if an ASBO is breached?

It is a criminal offence to break the terms of an ASBO and this would go on a person's criminal record. If the person who has the ASBO against them doesn't comply with the terms of it, you can report it to the police, who can arrest them.

Can ASBOs be granted against anyone?

Yes. It doesn't matter where you live, whether you own your house or are renting it from the council, a housing association or a private landlord, an ASBO can be granted against anyone who is causing a problem in your area. The person causing a problem doesn't have to live in your area and ASBOs can be granted against people who don't have a fixed address.

ASBOs can be made against children as young as ten years old. If an ASBO is made against a child under the age of 18, extra support can be ordered (eg providing counselling to deal with substance use or behavioural problems).

Who can apply for an ASBO?

Only the council or a registered social landlord (ie a housing association) can apply for an ASBO, so you need to report any problems to them first of all so they have a record of what's been happening. Most councils now have dedicated antisocial behaviour teams.

You can ask the council or housing association to apply for an ASBO, although they may not think it is appropriate and are not required to do so.

The council or registered social landlord must speak to the police before they apply for an ASBO. And if a registered social landlord is applying for an ASBO, they have to inform the council first as well.

The person who is accused of behaving in an antisocial manner can appeal against the application for an ASBO.

Can I apply for an ASBO against someone myself?

No. Although ASBOs can help to improve the community you live in, you can't actually apply for an ASBO yourself. Only councils and registered social landlords can do so.

Civil Court Action

A restraining order can be applied for via the civil courts. A restraining order is a set of rules set by the court, that the perpetrator has to abide by. For example the order may stop somebody entering a particular location or acting in a particular manner. The protection from harassment act 1997 is the legislation that can protect you. In order to access this form of protection you need to make an appointment with an experienced and sympathetic solicitor.

7

**YOUR
HEALTH
AND
EMOTIONAL
RESPONSES**

7 Your health and emotional responses

Being the victim of repeated bullying and hate crime is a stressful, unhealthy experience. Continued abuse impacts not only on your health, but it also affects your daily activities, your relationships with others and the way in which you perceive the world and its daily experiences. This chapter focuses on real achievable holistic health care advice, and places you in the centre. The following sections focus on your physical/emotional and spiritual health. Not all practices may be applicable to you, however feel free to pick and choose a number of practices that you feel comfortable with. Gradually with time, a number of these activities may form the basis of your new life, ensuring that you can cope with minor setbacks, daily stresses and bring health and happiness to yourself and loved ones. The last section of this chapter is an informative in depth review of Counselling Therapies, Post Traumatic Stress Disorder and Drug and Alcohol Treatments.

Looking after your physical body

Exercise

Exercise has been proven to lift your mood. You do not have to be super fit as 20 minutes a day is all you need to do. Start slowly and build yourself up.

Seek medical attention

If you have been assaulted, seek medical attention at the earliest opportunity. Take advice from your Doctor/Health Visitor/Midwife.

Try to reduce drinking alcohol

Alcohol is a depressant and will make you feel more depressed the next day. Using alcohol to solve your problems will inevitably lead to further feelings of despair.

Eat regular meals

Eat regular meals that are well balanced and contain the correct nutrients. Breakfast, lunch and tea. Skipping meals adds to fatigue and stress.

Take time off when sick

It's important to rest when we are ill.

Relax

Do not add to your busy life. A good old fashioned day off is just what the doctor ordered. Do the things that comfort you; take a nice hot bath, read a book, eat chocolate, or have a massage.

Take a mini-holiday

Getting away from your troubles will allow you to reflect differently. The solution to life's troubles is sometimes right under our noses and focusing on something else helps us to see things differently.

Get a good night's sleep

After a good night's sleep we begin the day in a better frame of mind. Try and keep to the same routine. Go to bed at 10 pm and rise at about 7 am.

Looking after your psychological self

Use visualization as a coping tool

When your abuser is particularly nasty visualise them standing as a small clown with a big red nose. Use any type of visualization that helps you make light of a situation.

Make time for self reflection

Write in a journal, draw a picture, consider your inner experiences – listen to your thoughts, judgements, beliefs, attitudes and feelings.

Happiness list

Make a list of all the things that make you feel happy. Carry the list with you and read it once in a while. Focus on the feeling of happiness. Do the things that make you feel happy and treat yourself.

Help others

Helping others helps you. By making someone else's life more pleasurable you gain friendship, support, skills, respect and new opportunities.

Looking after your emotions

Have fun

Be spontaneous and decide to do something new; push your boundaries and enjoy the moment.

Look after your pet

You do not have to own your own pet instead you could walk a neighbour's dog or go and help at the local cattery. Animals offer so much happiness.

Meet new people or start a new hobby

The old saying "A change is as good as a rest" is certainly true. A new direction in life can offer new opportunities. Education is an attitude of mind and helps to broaden your experiences. Look in your local library or town hall. Research groups at your local community centre.

Play music

Classical music works on different levels and has a soothing effect on your mind, body and soul. The power of music is astonishing.

Write poetry

Writing poetry allows us to express our inner feelings and helps us make sense of our world.

Allow yourself to cry

Emotions are best expressed, this can be particularly difficult if you're a man. Crying allows pent up frustrations to be released and can actually improve your inner feelings.

Find things that make you laugh

Humour is an age old anti-dote.

Visit your friends and family

Being around the people who matter to us helps us to reaffirm who we are and what we stand for. Visiting the people who care for us gives us an opportunity to talk and express ourselves.

Re-read favourite books, re-view favourite films

Re-living our inner feelings of happiness allows us to take a break from our current problems.

Give your self praise

Write down the things you do well, in one word describe these qualities.

Looking after yourself spiritually

Start the day with meditation

Your perception of the world starts with you. Starting the day with a clear mind allows you to concentrate and listen clearer. Qualities such as patience, calmness and tolerance develop. By becoming more centred you co-operate and have the ability to choose your responses to difficult situations.

Walk in the country

The green pastures of the countryside relax and soothe us, and combining the elements with exercise will rejuvenate you. The peace and tranquility of nature has a calming effect.

Thinking about suicide

Repeated bullying and hate crime effects our innate sense of identity. The sense of who we are. Whilst the weeks pass, the behaviour of the abuser changes. You become threatened, ridiculed, embarrassed, assaulted, isolated and targeted. Whilst this wave of pressure and stress grips us, our emotions and thoughts become heightened. When we wake in the morning, worry and anxiety can dominate us. Our thoughts cycle and we begin to think: What if? Why me? What have I done to deserve this? Stop, please stop. I can't cope any more. This endless stream of thought cycles around and around our minds. With all this thinking our emotional selves link with our thought patterns. The emotion of fear, of despair, of depression and sadness surface. This raging torrent of thinking and emotion engulf our inner world. Such a burden to carry. In these trying times it is absolutely normal to think and consider suicide. Our sense of identity is being eroded and our emotional world is being bombarded with feelings of sadness and anger. As human beings it is totally natural to want to avoid negative thoughts and emotions. When we are in the grip of these emotions, they literally blind us and we do not have the ability to see past the pain and frustration. We project those feelings onto our experience, convincing ourselves that we cannot solve our problem and that it will get worse. In the teachings of mindfulness, the avoidance of negative thoughts and emotions is known as aversion. Suicide is the final act of aversion. Step back and consider your true nature. By reading this book you have developed the knowledge to reduce the likelihood of violence, to engage with different methods, to develop inner peace and use the criminal justice system to its full protective capacity. The person who does this is not hopeless and helpless. You are resilient and courageous and your current situation will improve.

The intensity of your current thoughts and feelings in comparison to the whole of your life are small. The negative emotions that you are feeling are only minor turbulences when compared to span of your whole life. You have dreams, ideas, talents, companions, family members, experiences, support, pets and these are rich with life and vitality. It is okay to feel upset and angry and it's ok to feel that life is not fair. This negative experience will change and will not last forever.

What happens if you go ahead with suicide?

Sometimes the person who attempts suicide does not die but damages their body so badly that full recovery is impossible. If you take your own life, there is no turning back, no second chance. Death is final. It can be extremely traumatic for the person who finds your body. Something they will never forget. The effect of suicide on family and friends can be overwhelming. Of all the different ways of dying, suicide is the most difficult to deal with for those who are left behind - whether they are parents, children, partners, brothers, sisters, friends or even acquaintances.

So what can you do about it?

1. Share it

Tell someone else how you are feeling - a member of your family, your doctor, a teacher, school nurse, college counsellor, friend, someone from your church …..
If the person you are telling doesn't seem to understand, don't be put off - tell someone else. Phone the PAPYRUS helpline HOPELineUK 0800 068 41 41 Your call is confidential and you don't have to disclose your identity.

If you reach a suicidal crisis where the desire to kill yourself is overwhelming, you must tell someone. Ask them to keep you company until the feelings pass.

If you find it difficult to talk, write it down - send a letter, an email or a text.

Use the internet wisely by going only on websites that give positive help and hope for the future. Be very careful when speaking to people in chatrooms - you may be encouraged to go ahead and take your own life.

2. Deal with bad thoughts

Thinking bad thoughts about yourself all the time (especially about killing yourself) makes you feel worse. Tell someone you trust about your bad thoughts. Saying them out loud for the first time is scary but they will become less frightening the more you speak about them.

Try to recognise when your bad thoughts are likely to come and prepare for them. Try to find something that will get rid of them or will make you think about them less often. You could try being active, being with people or doing something you enjoy (even though you might not feel like it).

Just thinking about your bad thoughts a bit less often can be a great achievement. It can help you realise that you are starting to win the battle.

3. Get specialist help

Don't be afraid of going to see a specialist such as a counsellor or psychiatrist. You may want to take someone with you for company. Your family and friends can be very important in helping you get through this - think about allowing them to get involved in your treatment. There are some very good 'talking treatments' which work really well, especially if you go in the early days of feeling unwell. If you are not able to relate to the person you are seeing - ask to see someone else.

4. Understand your medication

If you have been given medication (tablets) to help with your suicidal feelings, make sure you understand how long it takes before they start having an effect. If they don't seem to be working, tell your doctor so they can try something else. Don't stop taking them because you feel better or because you are having side effects.

Get advice from your doctor first. You can also talk to the pharmacist about your medication.

5. Steer clear of alcohol and drugs

Although at first they give you a lift, they can make depressed people feel even worse in the long run. Under their influence you may do things or make decisions you would not normally make. Using alcohol and / or other drugs - including cannabis - can actually make some people suicidal.

6. Don't take risks

You may be feeling ambivalent about whether you live or die. In this frame of mind people sometimes take chances and do things on purpose which put their lives at risk, for example; driving the car in a way that could kill you (or someone else) or not taking an essential medication. Don't be pressured by other people into doing risky things either.

Be aware of the danger of making an impulsive, spur of the moment decision to kill yourself. This is more likely if something upsetting happens which you feel is the 'last straw', if you are angry or if you've been drinking or taking drugs.

Don't listen to sad music when you're really down. Playing it over and over again can compound suicidal feelings.

7. Take positive action

It may require huge effort but start looking after yourself with regular meals and plenty of exercise. Get out into the daylight and try to stay out of bed until night time. Find something to do which gives some structure to your day. Consider re-reading the chapter

The PAPYRUS helpline HOPELineUK 0800 068 41 41 begin_of_the_skype_ highlighting is there to help you. We know that some people find it difficult to pick up the phone. Please call - you have nothing to lose and everything to gain.

Post Traumatic Stress Disorder

In our everyday lives, any of us can have an experience that is overwhelming, frightening, and beyond our control. Most people, in time, get over experiences like this without needing help. In some people though, traumatic experiences set off a reaction that can last for many months or years. This is called Post- Traumatic Stress Disorder, or PTSD for short.

People who have repeatedly experienced:

- ❑ severe neglect or abuse as an adult or as a child
- ❑ severe repeated violence of abuse as an adult, e.g. torture, abusive imprisonment

can have a similar set of reactions. This is called 'complex PTSD' and is described later in this chapter

How does PTSD start?

PTSD can start after any traumatic event. A traumatic event is one where we can see that we are in danger, our life is threatened, or where we see other people dying or being injured. Some typical traumatic events would be:

- ❏ violent personal assault (sexual assault, rape, physical attack, abuse, robbery, mugging) Even hearing about an the unexpected injury or violent death of a family member or close friend can start PTSD.

Even hearing about an the unexpected injury or violent death of a family member or close friend can start PTSD.

When does PTSD start?

The symptoms of PTSD can start after a delay of weeks, or even months. They usually appear within 6 months of a traumatic event.

What does PTSD feel like?

Many people feel grief-stricken, depressed, anxious, guilty and angry after a traumatic experience. As well as these understandable emotional reactions, there are three main types of symptoms produced by such an experience:

1. Flashbacks & Nightmares

You find yourself re-living the event, again and again. This can happen both as a "flashback" in the day, and as nightmares when you are asleep. These can be so realistic that it feels as though you are living through the experience all over again. You see it in your mind, but may also feel the emotions and physical sensations of what happened - fear, sweating, smells, sounds, pain.

Ordinary things can trigger off flashbacks. For instance, if you had a car crash in the rain, a rainy day might start a flashback.

It may be so real that you actually believe that your abuser is sitting next to you.

2. Avoidance & Numbing

It can be just too upsetting to re-live your experience over and over again. So you distract yourself. You keep your mind busy by losing yourself in a hobby, working very hard, or spending your time absorbed in crossword or jigsaw puzzles. You avoid places and people that remind you of the trauma, and try not to talk about it.

You may deal with the pain of your feelings by trying to feel nothing at all - by becoming emotionally numb. You communicate less with other people, who then find it hard to live or work with you.

3. Being "On Guard"

You find that you stay alert all the time, as if you are looking out for danger. You can't relax. This is called "hypervigilance". You feel anxious and find it hard to sleep. Other people will notice that you are jumpy and irritable.

Other Symptoms

Emotional reactions to stress are often accompanied by:

- ❏ muscle aches and pains
- ❏ diarrhoea
- ❏ irregular heartbeats
- ❏ headaches
- ❏ feelings of panic and fear
- ❏ depression
- ❏ drinking too much alcohol
- ❏ using drugs (including painkillers).

Why are traumatic events so shocking?

They undermine our sense that life is fair, reasonably safe, and that we are secure. A traumatic experience makes it very clear that we can die at any time. The symptoms of PTSD are part of a normal reaction to narrowly avoided death.

Does everyone get PTSD after a traumatic experience?

No. But nearly everyone will have the symptoms of post traumatic stress for the first month or so. This is because they help to keep you going, and help you to understand the experience you have been through. This is an "acute stress reaction". Over a few weeks, most people slowly come to terms with what has happened, and their stress symptoms start to disappear.

Not everyone is so lucky. About 1 in 3 people will find that their symptoms just carry on and that they can't come to terms with what has happened. It is as though the process has got stuck. The symptoms of post traumatic stress, although normal in themselves, become a problem - or Post Traumatic Stress Disorder - when they go on for too long.

What makes PTSD worse?

The more disturbing the experience, the more likely you are to develop PTSD. The most traumatic events:

- ❏ are sudden and unexpected
- ❏ go on for a long time

- ❏ you are trapped and can't get away
- ❏ involve children.

If you are in a situation where you continue to be exposed to stress and uncertainty, this will make it difficult or impossible for your PTSD symptoms to improve.

What about ordinary "stress"?

Everybody feels stressed from time to time. Unfortunately, the word "stress" is used to mean two rather different things:

- ❏ our inner sense of worry, feeling tense or feeling burdened. or
- ❏ the problems in our life that are giving us these feelings. This could be

work, relationships, maybe just trying to get by without much money. Unlike PTSD, these things are with us, day in and day out. They are part of normal, everyday life, but can produce anxiety, depression, tiredness, and headaches. They can also make some physical problems worse, such as stomach ulcers and skin problems. These are certainly troublesome, but they are not the same as PTSD.

Why does PTSD happen?

We don't know for certain. There are a several possible explanations for why PTSD occurs.

Psychological

When we are frightened, we remember things very clearly. Although it can be distressing to remember these things, it can help us to understand what happened and, in the long run, help us to survive.

- ❏ The flashbacks, or replays, force us to think about what has happened. We can decide what to do if it happens again. After a while, we learn to think about it without becoming upset.
- ❏ It is tiring and distressing to remember a trauma. Avoidance and numbing keep the number of replays down to a manageable level.
- ❏ Being "on guard" means that we can react quickly if another crisis happens.

But we don't want to spend the rest of our life going over it. We only want to think about it when we have to - if we find ourselves in a similar situation.

How do I know when I've got over a traumatic experience?

When you can:

- ❏ think about it without becoming distressed
- ❏ not feel constantly under threat

❑   not think about it at inappropriate times.

Why is PTSD often not recognised?

❑   None of us like to talk about upsetting events and feelings.

❑   We may not want to admit to having symptoms, because we don't wantto be thought of as weak or mentally unstable.

❑   Doctors and other professionals are human. They may feel
uncomfortable if we try to talk about gruesome or horrifying events.

❑   People with PTSD often find it easier to talk about the other problems that go along with it - headache, sleep problems, irritability, depression, tension, substance abuse, family or work-related problems.

How can I tell if I have PTSD?

Have you have experienced a traumatic event of the sort described at the start of this leaflet?

If you have, do you:

❑   have vivid memories, flashbacks or nightmares?

❑   avoid things that remind you of the event?

❑   feel emotionally numb at times?

❑   feel irritable and constantly on edge but can't see why?

❑   eat more than usual, or use more drink or drugs than usual?

❑   feel out of control of your mood?

❑   find it more difficult to get on with other people?

❑   have to keep very busy to cope?

❑   feel depressed or exhausted?

If it is less that 6 weeks since the traumatic event, and these experiences are slowly improving, they may be part of the normal process of adjustment.

If it is more than 6 weeks since the event, and these experiences don't seem to be getting better, it is worth talking it over with your doctor.

Children and PTSD

PTSD can develop at any age.

Younger children may have upsetting dreams of the actual trauma, which then change into nightmares of monsters. They often re-live the trauma in their play. For example, a child involved in a serious road traffic accident might re- enact the crash with toy cars, over and over again.

They may lose interest in things they used to enjoy. They may find it hard to believe that they will live long enough to grow up.

They often complain of stomach aches and headaches.

How can PTSD be helped?

Helping yourself

Do ....

- ❏   keep life as normal as possible
- ❏   get back to your usual routine
- ❏   talk about what happened to someone you trust
- ❏   try relaxation exercises
- ❏   go back to work
- ❏   eat and exercise regularly
- ❏   go back to where the traumatic event happened
- ❏   take time to be with family and friends
- ❏   drive with care - your concentration may be poor
- ❏   be more careful generally - accidents are more likely at this time
- ❏   speak to a doctor
- ❏   expect to get better.

Don't ....

- ❏   beat yourself up about it - PTSD symptoms are not a sign of weakness. They are a normal reaction, of normal people, to terrifying experiences
- ❏   bottle up your feelings. If you have developed PTSD symptoms, don't keep it to yourself because treatment is usually very successful.
- ❏   avoid talking about it.
- ❏   expect the memories to go away immediately, they may be with you for quite some time.
- ❏   expect too much of yourself. Cut yourself a bit of slack while you adjust to what has happened.
- ❏   stay away from other people.
- ❏   drink lots of alcohol or coffee or smoke more.
- ❏   get overtired.
- ❏   miss meals.
- ❏   take holidays on your own.

What can interfere with getting better?

You may find that other people will:

- ❑ not let you talk about it
- ❑ avoid you
- ❑ be angry with you
- ❑ think of you as weak
- ❑ blame you

These are all ways in which other people protect themselves from thinking about gruesome or horrifying events. It won't help you because it doesn't give you the chance to talk over what has happened to you.

You may not be able to talk easily about it. A traumatic event can put you into a trance-like state which makes the situation seem unreal or bewildering. It is harder to deal with if you can't remember what happened, can't put it into words, or can't make sense of it.

Treatment

Just as there are both physical and psychological aspects to PTSD, so there are both physical and psychological treatments for it.

Psychotherapy

All the effective psychotherapies for PTSD focus on the traumatic experiences that have produced your symptoms rather than your past life. You cannot change or forget what has happened. You can learn to think differently about it, about the world, and about your life.

You need to be able to remember what happened, as fully as possible, without being overwhelmed by fear and distress. These therapies help you to put words to the traumatic experiences that you have had. By remembering the event, going over it and making sense of it, your mind can do its normal job, of storing the memories away and moving on to other things.

If you can start to feel safe again and in control of your feelings, you won't need to avoid the memories as much. Indeed, you can gain more control over your memories so that you only think about them when you want to, rather than having them erupt into your mind spontaneously.

All these treatments should all be given by specialists in the treatment of PTSD. The sessions should be at least weekly, every week, with the same therapist, and should usually continue for 8-12 weeks. Although sessions will usually last around an hour, they may sometimes last up to 90 minutes.

Cognitive Behavioural Therapy (CBT) is a way of helping you to think differently about your memories, so that they become less distressing and more manageable. It will usually also involve some relaxation work to help you tolerate the discomfort of thinking about the traumatic events.

EMDR (Eye Movement Desensitisation & Reprocessing) is a technique which uses eye movements to help the brain to process flashbacks and to make sense of the traumatic experience. It may sound odd, but it has been shown to work. Within the sphere of treating trauma, this technique is regarded as the most effective.

Group therapy involves meeting with a group of other people who have been through the same, or a similar traumatic event. The fact that other people in the group do have some idea of what you have been through can make it much easier to talk about what has happened.

Medication

SSRI antidepressant tablets will both reduce the strength of PTSD symptoms and relieve any depression that is also present. They will need to be prescribed by a doctor.

This type of medication should not make you sleepy, although they all have some side-effects in some people. They may also produce unpleasant symptoms if stopped quickly, so the dose should usually be reduced gradually. If they are helpful, you should carry on taking them for around 12 months. Soon after starting an antidepressany, some people may find that they feel more:

❑   anxious
❑   restless
❑   suicidal

Occasionally, if someone is so distressed that they cannot sleep or think clearly, anxiety-reducing medication may be necessary. These tablets should usually not be prescribed for more than 10 days or so.

Body-focussed Therapies

These can help to control the distress of PTSD. They can also reduce hyperarousal, or the feeling of being "on guard" all the time. These therapies include physiotherapy and osteopathy, but also complementary therapies such as massage, acupuncture, reflexology, yoga, meditation and tai chi. They all help you to develop ways of relaxing and managing stress.

Effectiveness of Treatments

At present, there is evidence that EMDR, cognitive behavioural therapy and antidepressants are all effective. There is not enough information for us to say that one of these treatments is better than another. There is no evidence that other forms of psychotherapy or counselling are helpful to PTSD.

Complex PTSD

This can start weeks or months after the traumatic event, but may take years to be recognised for what they are. As well as the symptoms of PTSD described above, you may:

- ❏ feel shame and guilt
- ❏ have a sense of numbness, a lack of feelings in your body
- ❏ be unable to enjoy anything
- ❏ control your emotions by using street drugs, alcohol, or by harmingyourself
- ❏ cut yourself off from what is going on around you (dissociation)
- ❏ have physical symptoms caused by your distress
- ❏ find that you can't put your emotions into words
- ❏ want to kill yourself
- ❏ take risks and do things on the 'spur of the moment'.

What makes PTSD worse?

If:

- ❏ it happens at an early stage - the earlier the age, the worse the trauma
- ❏ it is caused by a parent or other care giver
- ❏ the trauma is severe
- ❏ the trauma goes on for a long time
- ❏ you are isolated
- ❏ you are still in touch with the abuser and/or threats to your safety.

How does it come about?

The earlier the trauma happens, the more it affects psychological development. Some children cope by being defensive or aggressive, while others cut themselves off from what is going on around them. They tend to grow up with a sense of shame and guilt rather than feeling confident and good about themselves.

Getting better

Try to start doing the normal things of life that have nothing to do with your past experiences of trauma. This could include finding friends, getting a job, doing regular exercise, learning relaxation techniques, developing a hobby or having pets. This helps you slowly to trust the world around you.

Lack of trust in other people - and the world in general - is central to complex PTSD. Treatment often needs to be longer to allow you to develop a secure relationship with a therapist - if you like, to experience that it is possible to trust someone in this world without being abused. The work will often happen in 3 stages:

Stabilisation

You learn how to understand and control your distress and emotional cutting off, or 'dissociation'. This can involve 'grounding' techniques to help you stay in the present - concentrating on ordinary physical feelings that remind you that you are not still living in the traumatic past.

You may also be able to 'disconnect' your physical symptoms of fear and anxiety from the memories and emotions that produce them, making them less frightening.

You start to be able to tolerate day to day life without experiencing anxiety and flashbacks. This may sometimes be the only help that is needed.

Trauma-focused Therapy

EMDR or CBT (see above) can help you remember your traumatic experiences with less distress and more control. Other psychotherapies, including psychodynamic psychotherapy, can also be helpful. Care needs to be taken in complex PTSD because these treatments can make the situation worse if not used properly.

Reintegration

You begin to develop a new life for yourself. You become able to use your skills or learn new ones and to make satisfying relationships in the real world.

Medication can be used if you feel too distressed or unsafe, or if psychotherapy is not possible. It can include both antidepressants and antipsychotioc medication - but not usually tranquillisers or sleeping tablets.

WHAT IS CBT?

It is a way of talking about:

- ❑ How you think about yourself, the world and other people
- ❑ How what you do affects your thoughts and feelings.

CBT can help you to change how you think ("Cognitive") and what you do ("Behaviour"). These changes can help you to feel better. Unlike some of the other talking treatments, it focuses on the "here and now" problems and difficulties. Instead of focussing on the causes of your distress or symptoms in the past, it looks for ways to improve your state of mind now.

It has been found to be helpful in Anxiety, Depression, Panic, Agoraphobia and other phobias, Social phobia, Bulimia, Obsessive compulsive disorder, Post traumatic stress disorder and Schizophrenia

How does it work?

CBT can help you to make sense of overwhelming problems by breaking them down into smaller parts. This makes it easier to see how they are connected and how they affect you. These parts are:

❑ A Situation - a problem, event or difficult situation

From this can follow:

❑ Thoughts
❑ Emotions
❑ Physical feelings
❑ Actions

Each of these areas can affect the others. How you think about a problem can affect how you feel physically and emotionally. It can also alter what you do about it. There are helpful and unhelpful ways of reacting to most situations, depending on how you think about them.

The same situation has led to two very different results, depending on how you thought about the situation. How you **think** has affected how you **felt** and what you **did**. In the example in the left hand column, you've jumped to a conclusion without very much evidence for it - and this matters, because it's led to:

❑ a number of uncomfortable feelings
❑ an unhelpful behaviour.

Example:

		Unhelpful	Helpful
Situation:	You've had a bad day, feel fed up, so go out shopping. As you walk down the road, someone you know walks by and, apparently, ignores you.		
Thoughts:		He/she ignored me - they don't like me	He/she looks a bit wrapped up in themselves - I wonder if there's something wrong?
Emotional:		Low, sad and rejected	Concerned for the other person
Feelings			
Physical:		Stomach cramps, low energy, feel sick	None - feel comfortable
Action:		Go home and avoid them	Get in touch to make sure they're OK

If you go home feeling depressed, you'll probably brood on what has happened and feel worse. If you get in touch with the other person, there's a good chance you'll feel better about yourself. If you don't, you won't have the chance to correct any misunderstandings about what they think of you - and you will probably feel worse. This is a simplified way of looking at what happens. The whole sequence, and parts of it, can also feedback like this:

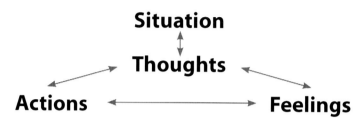

This "vicious circle" can make you feel worse. It can even create new situations that make you feel worse. You can start to believe quite unrealistic (and unpleasant) things about yourself. This happens because, when we are distressed, we are more likely to jump to conclusions and to interpret things in extreme and unhelpful ways.

CBT can help you to break this vicious circle of altered thinking, feelings and behaviour. When you see the parts of the sequence clearly, you can change them - and so change the way you feel. CBT aims to get you to a point where you can "do it yourself", and work out your own ways of tackling these problems.

"Five areas" assessment

This is another way of connecting all the 5 areas mentioned above. It builds in our relationships with other people and helps us to see how these can make us feel better or worse. Other issues such as debt, job and housing difficulties are also important. If you improve one area, you are likely to improve other parts of your life as well.

What does CBT involve?

The sessions

CBT can be done individually or with a group of people. It can also be done from a self-help book or computer programme. In England and Wales two computer-based programmes have been approved for use by the NHS. Fear Fighter is for people with phobias or panic attacks, Beating the Blues is for people with mild to moderate depression.

If you have individual therapy:

❑   You will usually meet with a therapist for between 5 and 20, weekly, or fortnightly, sessions. Each session will last between 30 and 60 minutes.

❑   In the first 2-4 sessions, the therapist will check that you can use this sort of treatment and you will check that you feel comfortable with it.

- ❑ The therapist will also ask you questions about your past life and background. Although CBT concentrates on the here and now, at times you may need to talk about the past to understand how it is affecting you now.
- ❑ You decide what you want to deal with in the short, medium and long term.
- ❑ You and the therapist will usually start by agreeing on what to discuss that day.

The work

- ❑ With the therapist, you break each problem down into its separate parts, as in the example above. To help this process, your therapist may ask you to keep a diary. This will help you to identify your individual patterns of thoughts, emotions, bodily feelings and actions.
- ❑ Together you will look at your thoughts, feelings and behaviours to work out:
  - if they are unrealistic or unhelpful
  - how they affect each other, and you.
- ❑ The therapist will then help you to work out how to change unhelpful thoughts and behaviours
- ❑ It's easy to talk about doing something, much harder to actually do it. So, after you have identified what you can change, your therapist will recommend "homework" - you practise these changes in your everyday life. Depending on the situation, you might start to:
- ❑ Question a self-critical or upsetting thought and replace it with a positive (and more realistic) one that you have developed in CBT
- ❑ recognise that you are about to do something that will make you feel worse and, instead, do something more helpful.
- ❑ At each meeting you discuss how you've got on since the last session. Your therapist can help with suggestions if any of the tasks seem too hard or don't seem to be helping.
- ❑ They will not ask you to do things you don't want to do - you decide the pace of the treatment and what you will and won't try. The strength of CBT is that you can continue to practise and develop your skills even after the sessions have finished. This makes it less likely that your symptoms or problems will return.

How effective is CBT?

- ❑ It is one of the most effective treatments for conditions where anxiety or depression is the main problem
- ❑ It is the most effective psychological treatment for moderate and severe depression
- ❑ It is as effective as antidepressants for many types of depression

What other treatments are there and how do they compare?

CBT is used in many conditions, so it isn't possible to list them all in this leaflet. We will look at alternatives to the most common problems - anxiety and depression.

- ❏ CBT isn't for everyone and another type of talking treatment may work better for you.
- ❏ CBT is as effective as antidepressants for many forms of depression. It may be slightly more effective than antidepressants in treating anxiety.
- ❏ For severe depression, CBT should be used with antidepressant medication. When you are very low you may find it hard to change the way you think until antidepressants have started to make you feel better.
- ❏ Tranquillisers should not be used as a long term treatment for anxiety. CBT is a better option.

Problems with CBT

- ❏ If you are feeling low and are having difficulty concentrating, it can be hard, at first, to get the hang of CBT - or, indeed, any psychotherapy
- ❏ This may make you feel disappointed or overwhelmed. A good therapist will pace your sessions so you can cope with the work you are trying to do
- ❏ It can sometimes be difficult to talk about feelings of depression, anxiety, shame or anger

How long will the treatment last?

A course may be from 6 weeks to 6 months. It will depend on the type of problem and how it is working for you. The availability of CBT varies between different areas and there may be a waiting list for treatment.

What if the symptoms come back?

There is always a risk that the anxiety or depression will return. If they do, your CBT skills should make it easier for you to control them. So, it is important to keep practising your CBT skills, even after you are feeling better.

There is some research that suggests CBT may be better than antidepressants at preventing depression coming back. If necessary, you can have a "refresher" course.

So what impact would CBT have on my life?

Depression and anxiety are unpleasant. They can seriously affect your ability to work and enjoy life. CBT can help you to control the symptoms. It is unlikely to have a negative effect on your life, apart from the time you need to give up to do it.

There are many different types of psychotherapy. They are all ways of helping people to overcome stress, emotional problems, relationship problems or troublesome habits. What they have in common is that they are all treatments based on talking to another person and sometimes doing things together. They are the "talking treatments". The person carrying out the treatment is usually called a therapist, the person being seen is usually referred to as the client.

Psychodynamic psychotherapy

This focuses on the feelings we have about other people, especially our family and those we are close to. Treatment involves discussing past experiences and how these may have led to our present situation and also how these past experiences may be affecting our life now. The understanding gained frees the person to make choices about what happens in the future.

Psychodynamic psychotherapy may involve quite brief therapy for specific difficulties. If your problems are long-standing, treatment may mean attending regular sessions over many months.

Behavioural psychotherapy

This tries to change patterns of behaviour more directly. Patients can be helped to overcome fears by spending more and more time in the situation they fear, or by learning ways of reducing their anxiety. They may be given 'homework' exercises, and asked to keep diaries or to practice new skills between sessions.

Behavioural psychotherapy is particularly effective for anxiety, panic, phobias, obsessive-compulsive problems and various kinds of social or sexual difficulty. Relief from symptoms often occurs quite quickly.

Can these different approaches work together?

These are all very different sorts of treatment, but they all help us to understand better how we work, which can help us to make changes in our lives.

Psychotherapists may use a combination of techniques to suit the individual, and people may progress from say individual to group therapy, or marital work to individual treatment.

What actually happens?

Psychotherapy usually involves regular meetings at the same time, same place every week or two weeks. In most cases the length of the treatment will be agreed between the client(s) and the therapist(s) within a month or so of starting. What happens during a session is usually considered confidential to the people in that session.

In individual psychotherapy, one patient and one therapist talk together in a quiet room, usually for 50 minutes or so.

In group therapy, several people with similar sorts of problems meet regularly with a therapist or therapists. These sessions may be longer than in individual psychotherapy. Group therapy may appear less intimate, but it is not a cheap or second-rate treatment - in fact it is the best treatment for some problems. The experience of discovering one is not alone, and of being able to help other people, is powerfully encouraging and is often the first step towards getting better.

Counselling

Counselling takes place when a counsellor sees a client in a private and confidential setting to explore a difficulty the client is having, distress they may be experiencing or perhaps their dissatisfaction with life, or loss of a sense of direction and purpose. It is always at the request of the client as no one can properly be 'sent' for counselling.

Confidentiality may be examined if there is a serious danger of harm to someone - either the person or someone else, counsellors may consider whether it is necessary to discuss this with someone else (e.g. a G.P). Normal practice is for the counsellor to share their concern with the client concerned and for the client and counsellor together to consider what, if anything, it might be helpful to share, and with whom.

By listening attentively and patiently the counsellor can begin to perceive the difficulties from the client's point of view and can help them to see things more clearly, possibly from a different perspective.

Counselling is a way of enabling choice or change or of reducing confusion. It does not involve giving advice or directing a client to take a particular course of action. Counsellors do not judge or exploit their clients in any way.

In the counselling sessions the client can explore various aspects of their life and feelings, talking about them freely and openly in a way that is rarely possible with friends or family. Bottled up feelings such as anger, anxiety, grief and embarrassment can become very intense and counselling offers an opportunity to explore them, with the possibility of making them easier to understand. The counsellor will encourage the expression of feelings and as a result of their training will be able to accept and reflect the client's problems without becoming burdened by them.

Acceptance and respect for the client are essentials for a counsellor and, as the relationship develops, so too does trust between the counsellor and client, enabling the client to look at many aspects of their life, their relationships and themselves which they may not have considered or been able to face before.

The counsellor may help the client to examine in detail the behaviour or situations which are proving troublesome and to find an area where it would be possible to initiate some change as a start. The counsellor may help the client to look at the options open to them and help them to decide the best for them.

Counselling or psychotherapy training?

It is not possible to make a generally accepted distinction between counselling and psychotherapy. There are well founded traditions which use the terms interchangeably and others which distinguish between them. If there are differences, then they relate more to the individual psychotherapist's or counsellor's training and interests and to the setting in which they work, rather than to any intrinsic difference in the two activities. to offer therapeutic work which in any other context would be called psychotherapy.

What is meditation?

Meditation is the practice of focussing your mind on a positive, virtuous feeling. For example if you are feeling bitter and resentful and you focus your meditation on the feeling of love. After spending time concentrating on the feeling of love, your mind will feel more peaceful. Meditation has its origins in many of the world's religions. It is a technique and there is not a right way or wrong way to meditate. The goal of meditation is to train the mind to think more positively.

What are the benefits of meditation?

Meditation has been scrutinized by many scientific studies. It has been proven that the technique of meditation can reduce stress and improve relaxation.

How do I meditate?

Meditate in a clear and quiet place. Do not rush straight into the meditation but spend a few moments to relax into a comfortable posture with your back straight but not tense. Always begin by developing a positive wish to benefit yourself and others through your meditation. Try not to forget the objective meditation. The objective is the type of feeling you are trying to focus on. Before you rise from meditation, mentally dedicate the positive energy that you have created to yourself and others. Throughout the day try and recall the feeling of meditation as often as you can. Use it to guide everything you think, say and do. Spend twenty minutes each day meditating.

What can I expect?

The practice of meditation will take some time to master, and take each session slowly. Meditation is a skill that can be learnt. Like all skills you have to practice them daily. Do not be hard on yourself in the early days. You will get glimpses of a peaceful mind, however, with time and effort the experience of peace will lengthen.

An actual meditation – "Breathing Meditation"

Sit on a chair in quiet a room by yourself. Unplug the phone and give yourself twenty minutes of uninterrupted time. Keep your feet firmly on the floor. Place your hands in a cupped position and find a relaxed position with your back straight. Close your eyes. Take a deep breath and count in your head to the number four. Exhale with a long relaxed breath and count to the number six. Continue with this until you are feeling a little more relaxed. Spend five minutes breathing deeply. Thoughts will keep whizzing into your head. Don't try and stop them but let them come and go. Thoughts are like the tide; they come in and go out. Try not to let the tide sweep you out to sea. Continue to focus on your breath. As you inhale feel the cool air pass your nostrils, and as you exhale feel the warm air pass through your nostrils. Focus on the feelings of cold air and warm air. Continue breathing deeply for six counts and exhaling for six counts. Try and hold your concentration for five minutes. Within this breathing meditation we are aiming to focus on the feeling air. Relax and breathe. As you relax maintain your concentration.

As you inhale imagine the breath as white smoke entering your body, helping you and nourishing every cell in your body. As you exhale imagine thick black smoke leaving your body, making you more rejuvenated and stronger. Imagine that you are slowly cleansing your mind. Visualise your pure heart and feel at peace with yourself. Slowly resume by concentrating on your breath, enjoying that space of calm and happiness. Open your eyes."

A meditation to oppose anger - focussing and harvesting a loving mind meditation

Sit on a chair in a quiet room by yourself. Unplug the phone and give yourself twenty minutes of uninterrupted time. Keep your feet firmly on the floor. Place your hands in a cupped position and find a relaxed position with your back straight. Close your eyes. Take a deep breath and count in your head to the number four. Exhale with a long relaxed breath and count to the number six. Continue with this until you are feeling a little more relaxed. Spend five minutes breathing deeply. Today there are many people who exist to benefit you and do so to ensure all your happiness. Believe it or not, but kindness is all around us. Every act that a person does has at the heart of it an act of kindness or goodness. Starting with you, I want you to consider the kindness that you have received. As you read through the following descriptions I want you to think about your own life and feel each person's happiness. The clothes you are wearing were the result of someone else's happiness. Many people were involved in making the clothes in harsher conditions than you are living in. Roads were built to help transport the clothes. The roads were built by hard physical work in very demanding circumstances. The labourers were working for their happiness and yours. Eventually the clothes were displayed in a shop. You were given money so that you could purchase them. The room you are sitting in was constructed to provide your family with shelter and security. The architect, the builder, the carpenter, the plasterer all co- operated to provide you with this basic need. The meal you ate last passed through many hands before you ate it. The farmer, the packager, the cook all worked together to feed you. They did this to provide happiness to themselves and others. Happiness is born out of love. The book you are reading was given to you as others want you to be happy. Your family spent hours teaching you to read and sent you to school. The teacher taught you many skills so that you can co-operate in this world. All your daily needs have been taken care of. Somebody somewhere has considered your problems and has provided a solution to your suffering. We have central heating, clean sanitation, medicines, charities, transportation, education, music, etc. All that is around us has been provided by many people. Indeed I have written this book as I genuinely want you to be happy. Focus on feeling and understanding that others have acted as a result of love. As you visualise all this kindness focus on the feeling of love that is developing in your heart. Now keep and hold the feeling of love within your heart until it begins to fade away. As it fades away remind yourself about how many people have benefited you and acted out of love, once again focus and concentrate on the feeling of love. As you rise out of the meditation return to focussing on your breath, imagine all your anger slowly rising in the air as thick black smoke. As you take a breath imagine pure light entering every part of your body.

A Meditation To Heal Life's Problems

This powerful meditation is also know as "taking and giving". It is a meditation that heals and restores. "I want you to imagine in your mind all the problems, anxieties and fears that you have about the bullying that you are experiencing. Picture the people, circumstances and situations clearly. Remind yourself about the hurt that you have been feeling and the emotions that have accumulated in your heavy heart. Now imagine rising above all this hurt and clearly seeing all that has happened to you. Slowly imagine turning these visions into thick black smoke. As you take a deep breath in, imagine all the black smoke entering your body. The smoke clears as it enters your heart and dissolves. Now as you exhale imagine sending rays of warm, pure light from your heart breaking all the unhappiness in the world. Send as much light to as many people as you can. Continue to use this visualisation as you breathe in and out. Focus your concentration on this meditation for as long as you can" There are many forms of meditation. Meditation can be used to improve your mental happiness. Try different styles of meditation and experiment with the one that suits your particular needs. Some styles focus on a particular religious aspect and others do not. It is entirely up to you.

What is Mindfulness Meditation?

Mindfulness Meditation is the practice of inner observation. Meditation is simply an inner investigative process of literally paying attention to inner feelings, thoughts, body sensations, touch, taste and smell. By turning inwards we are allowing ourselves to process, manage and make sense of what we are seeing and perceiving. We are allowing calm and relaxation to pervade our senses at any giving moment. This might be bodily sensations, such as tingling in your feet, an ache in your back, sounds around you, or various thoughts and emotions.

You accept and not judge whatever comes up. Watch without getting too involved. For example if you think 'This meditation is a waste of time', or 'I just can't do this' then you just observe these thoughts and any linked emotions such as fear and anxiety. Just keep watching.

How can mindfulness meditation protect us from depression?

Depression is triggered by identification with the negative thoughts, which endlessly cycle in the mind. This is known as 'rumination'. Mindfulness can help to loosen identification with these thoughts. To help you realise that you are not your thoughts. That they are transient, and will fade if you don't become involved with them. In fact practising mindfulness can make you a sort of expert on your own mind, so that you can spot negative thoughts before they take over. In an abusive relationship, this practice can have many benefits, your awareness will allow you to identify with your partner's behaviour patterns and how they affect you. This knowledge and space will give you time to think clearly and identify how manipulative your partner or ex-partner can be.

Mindfulness Meditation has been scientifically tested and the results of the program are validated and profound. Over 100 studies have been conducted. Mindfulness Meditation has shown to lower cardiac risk factors pertaining to heart disease and reduce the prevalence of depression and anxiety. In California, schools are using the program to de-stress students and the results have shown to improve school behaviour and improve concentration and learning outcomes.

How to practice mindfulness of thoughts and emotions

Mindfulness can be practised anywhere, while brushing your teeth or mowing the lawn, but the most useful place to start is probably during sitting meditation. When you meditate it's best to begin by establishing some stability in your mind by spending a few minutes watching your breath. You can then move on to observe the ebb and flow of your thoughts and emotions. It's best to spend just a few minutes on this before returning to the breath again.

Jon Kabat Zinn, author of 'Full Catastrophe Living', explains how to practise mindfulness meditation of thoughts and emotions as follows:

1. When your attention is relatively stable on the breath, shift your awareness to the process of thinking itself. And just watch thoughts come into your field of attention. Try to perceive them as events in your mind.

2. Note their content and charge while if possible not being drawn into thinking about them.

3. Note that an individual thought does not last long, it is impermanent. If it comes, it will go. Be aware of this.

4. Note how some thoughts keep coming back.

5. Note those thoughts that are 'I', 'me' or 'mine' thoughts, observing carefully how 'you', the non-judging observer, feel about them.

6. Note when the mind creates a 'self' to be preoccupied with how well or badly your life is going.

7. Note thoughts about the past and thoughts about the future.

8. Note thoughts about greed, wanting, grasping, clinging.

9. Note thoughts about anger, disliking, hatred, aversion, rejection.

10. Note feelings and moods as they come and go.

11. Note feelings associated with different thought contents.

12. If you get lost in all of this just get back to your breathing.

If you would like to learn mindfulness from the comfort of your own home you can now purchase a mindfulness programme online from **www.bemindfulonline.com**

Drug and alcohol healthcare

Many people who have experienced repeated bullying and hatecrime have also developed a need to use Drugs and Alcohol. Research confirms these fact's. You may have noticed a need to have a stiff drink after an unpleasant experience. After time the need to drink or use drugs has become a daily habit. There are many statutory and voluntary agencies that understand your experience and can help using various approaches. There are many reasons why some one uses substances: escapism, pain removal, coping ability and doing what others tell them.

Where can I get help?

A good website that lists all agencies in the UK is the Alcohol Concern Website: servicesdirectory.alcoholconcern.org.uk/
Talk to frank 0800 77 66 00 www.talktofrank.com
Drink line is also useful **0800 917 8282**
You may also find information from **NHS Direct, Citizen's Advice Bureau**

Approaching a Local Agency

When you walk through the door of a local agency, you will first be given an explanation of what the agency can offer you depending on your personal circumstances. The counsellor or therapist will sit down with you in a closed room, whereby you will be asked a number of questions. Confidentiality may be examined if there is a serious danger of harm to someone - either the person or someone else, counsellors may consider whether it is necessary to discuss this with someone else (e.g. a G.P). Normal practice is for the counsellor to share their concern with the client concerned and for the client and counsellor together to consider what, if anything, it might be helpful to share, and with whom. The questions will ask you about your personal life, your drinking / drugs habits and your willingness to participate in a programme of change. The counsellor will not expect you to have the answers and will listen and not judge your answers. Many counsellor's have had domestic violence training and are aware of your complex situation.

Once the counsellor has built a detailed picture of your current lifestyle and habits, the counsellor will design a care plan that suits your needs. You may be asked to sign a contract that summarises your individual care plan. If you are drinking or using heavily it is advisable not to stop drinking / using straight away. A slow reduction plan is generally followed.

What can I expect?

The methods used vary from agency to agency, however you may be offered a detailed 12 steps programme incorporating the following:

- ❏ One to One Counselling (Choice of male or female counsellor)
- ❏ Group Sessions (may not be appropriate for Domestic Violence)
- ❏ Medication (this may put you more danger, depending on the type of medication, if in doubt ask.)
- ❏ An education programme (understanding alcohol and drugs)
- ❏ Herbal Medication (helping you sleep, detoxification)
- ❏ Ear Acupuncture (helps to reduce stress and cravings)
- ❏ Out Reach Work (a worker will help you with needle exchange etc)
- ❏ Post Counselling Groups (A chance to support others)
- ❏ Other processes such as Cognitive Behavioral Therapy.

Useful Numbers

NHS Direct **0845 4647** www.nhsdirect.nhs.uk

British Association for Counselling and Psychotherapy
01455 883316 www.bacp.co.uk

Saneline for anyone concerned about their own mental health or that of someone else. Local rate helpline: **08457 678 000** 12 noon to 11pm Monday to Friday and 12 noon to 6pm on Saturday and Sunday. www.sane.org.uk

Samaritans provide a listening service for those in distress or considering suicide. **0845 790 9090** 24 hour helpline.

No Panic: **0808 808 0545** freephone for those suffering from anxiety disorders and panic attacks. Provides advice, counselling, befriending and refers to local services when available.

National self-harm network: www.nshn.co.uk For those who self-harm or for those supporting them. Gives information (and debunks myths) about self harm and lists organisations which provide support.

Papyrus Preventing Young Suicide
PAPYRUS helpline HOPELineUK 0800 068 41 41

Young Minds www.youngminds.org.uk
The Young Minds parents' information service provides support, information and help for parents concerned about a young person's mental health: 0800 018 2138. They also have a variety of leaflets and booklets, including one which explores how divorce and separation affect children and young people.

8

SCHOOL BULLYING AND RESTORATIVE JUSTICE

When I started to research school bullying I trawled through many school websites and read many school bullying policies. A school adopts its own policy according to its own experience. There is not much consistency from one school to the next. Some schools tackle the issue head on and others have a policy that appears flimsy and inadequate. As a parent it would be easy to blame a school for its shortcomings and it would be very easy to blame the school for your child's bullying problem. Bullying is all our problem and we can all contribute to its solution.

The community approach is one that involves problem solving and actively encourages all sections of the community to become involved. By adopting this approach you not only solve your child's problem, but actively make the school a safer place to study and work in. This approach will benefit your child's education, improve learning and benefit the wider community. If you are in the process of meeting the head teacher this may be an opportunity to raise the issues of the problem solving approach.

The community model adopts the theory of cause and effect. If the causes responsible for bullying are identified and reduced, then the overall effect of bullying is reduced. Many parents that I have helped over the years focus on the punishment aspect of this model. Punishment is seen by many as the answer to the bullying problem. If the bullying did not happen in the first instance, then I am sure there would be no one to punish.

For the community approach to work the various stakeholders need to understand what is required of them and what they need to do. Communication needs to be open and transparent. In many policing activities this model has been proven to work and reduce crime. Each stakeholder's actions are interdependent and contribute to a safer community. After all the stakeholders have been identified they must be given an opportunity to answer all the questions below. An action plan that is specific, measurable, achievable, realistic and set within a time period must be adopted and communicated to all.

The anti-bullying alliance have a range of publications that relate to school bullying and hate crime. Teachers may want to consider using their free and informative tool kits. The following paragraphs have been written for a wide range of stakeholders.

Focussing on the victim

❑ Has your child identified a pattern of when and where the bullying is occurring?

❑ Has your child identified a safety plan that minimises confrontational behaviour?

❑ Has your child's safety plan been incorporated into your child's daily school

- ❑ activities?

- ❑ Who has your child told?

- ❑ Has your child written an account of what has happened?

- ❑ Has your child been offered a counselling session?

- ❑ Does your child understand what effect personal safety has on their own welfare?

- ❑ Does your child have a good network of friends?

- ❑ Does your child carry a panic alarm or mobile phone?

- ❑ Have you limited your child's internet and mobile phone access?

- ❑ Has your child been offered assertiveness training?

- ❑ Has your child adapted social networking sites?

- ❑ Does your child attend school- or outside clubs?

- ❑ Are you considering sending your child to a self defence class?

- ❑ Has your child identified why they believe the bullying is occurring?

Focussing on the location of bullying; the school environment

- ❑ Has the school identified a list of Bullying Trouble Spots?

- ❑ How often are these Bullying Trouble Spots patrolled by school staff?

- ❑ Has each Bullying Trouble Spots been risk assessed? What potential for injury does this location have?

- ❑ Does the school have CCTV? Does the CCTV cover Bullying Trouble Spots?

- ❑ Does the school have mirrors that cover blind spots?

- ❑ Does the school have a Tannoy system?

- ❑ How do staff communicate when an incident occurs? Do staff carry radios?

- ❑ Have staff had violence and confrontation training?

- ❑ Are the streets adjoining the school covered by CCTV?

- ❏ Does the school have a school bag searching policy
- ❏ Does the school have metal detectors?

Focussing on the bully

- ❏ How are the bullies punished?
- ❏ What help are the bullies offered? Are they referred to a counsellor, anger management specialist or educational psychologist?
- ❏ Has the bully been offered diversionary activities that keep them away from the victim and his/her friends?
- ❏ Has the bully's class involvement been monitored?
- ❏ Have the bully's parents been contacted?
- ❏ Are there problems at home?
- ❏ What efforts have been made to separate your child?

Focussing on the bystander

The bystander is indeed part of the overall problem. Within sports psychology it is a well documented fact that the bystander can improve or motivate a performer into a more competitive state of mind. This is also called social facilitation. This same effect can be observed at football matches or outside nightclubs when violence occurs. In many cases social facilitation increases the risk of violence and harm. If we do not focus and re-educate the bystander then how can we begin to attempt to reduce violence on the streets of the UK? The bystander needs to understand this theory and take responsibility. Schools need to educate parents and children.

- ❏ Have the bystanders been identified?
- ❏ Has each bystander been interviewed?
- ❏ Has each bystander received an awareness input?
- ❏ Does the school punish bystanders?

Focussing on the parent

Prior to going to school you must do the following:

- ❏ Take a good look at your child. Is there anything that makes them an attractive target? Follow the advice in the chapter "Personal Safety"
- ❏ Does your child know its daily safety plan?

- [ ] Does your child fully understand the process of confrontation and reducing verbal bullying?

- [ ] Does your child know its self care plan?

- [ ] Give your child 15 minutes of quiet time; consider a simple breathing meditation

- [ ] Tell them that you love them and that you will do everything to help them Remind them to tell someone and report any incidents.

As a parent it is all too easy to go straight to the head teacher and demand the bullying to be stopped. I would advise parents to talk discreetly to as many school workers as possible. Consider informing the local school's community police officer, police community support officer, neighbourhood warden, classroom assistant or playground warden.

Focussing on the school response

- [ ] Is the issue of bullying incorporated into daily staff meetings?

- [ ] Does the school segregate year groups at playtime? Does each member of staff know which children are at risk?

- [ ] How are staff members informed about bullying?

- [ ] Who is designated as the school lead with regard to bullying?

- [ ] Which member of staff co-ordinates school patrols?

- [ ] What systems are in place to report bullying?

- [ ] How is bullying investigated by the school?

- [ ] Is there a gang culture at school?

- [ ] Is there a designated safe room at school (a place where children can de-stress and relax)?

- [ ] Does the school monitor social networking websites?

- [ ] Does your school have an acceptable behaviour contract?

- [ ] Does the school have a telling policy?

- [ ] Does the school have a peer support programme?

- [ ] Does the school keep a watchful eye at home time? Are children escorted on and off the premises?

- [ ] Does the school adopt restorative approaches?

Restorative approaches work to resolve conflict between individuals or groups and to repair harm. They encourage those who have caused harm to acknowledge the impact of what they have done and give them an opportunity to make reparation. They offer those who have suffered harm the opportunity to have their harm or loss acknowledged and amends made. Restorative approaches may not be suitable for all incidents of bullying.

Peer support programmes adopt a mentoring service to all children. Certain children are chosen and are trained to listen and support others. These may also be called "Buddy Programmes". This type of programme develops the buddy and the victim. Valuable skills are transferred, and the children feel valued and listened to.

'Telling schools" support the concept that bystanders should report bullying to the class teacher. This takes the onus away from the victim. It also takes away the fear of "telling tales". I support this approach because fundamentally it builds a sense of justice. Stepping aside from the school problem, if we cast our minds to the daily reports of serious crime within the media of the UK, we begin to realise that if it was not for witnesses coming forward to the police, supporting justice, then our efforts would be futile.

Focussing on partnership agencies and improving communication

❑   How often do the local police or police Community Support Officers patrol key trouble spots?

❑   Has the anti-bullying policy been shared with the community and local councils? What can they do to assist?

❑   Are all parents aware of the anti-bullying policy?

❑   How are other agencies involved in the anti-bullying policy?

❑   How are all concerns communicated?

NATIONAL BULLYING AND HATE CRIME SERVICES

Across the UK there are a number of highly experienced and long-standing agencies that deliver prevention, intervention or a combination of both practices. At the heart of your bullying experience are your particular needs. The agency that is supporting you, needs to know which particular needs are more important at the particular time of reporting the bullying incident.

For example, the abuser may be particularly dangerous and therefore your need for personal safety will far outweigh your need for emotional support at the time of reporting the incident. When reporting incidents to an agency ask yourself the following questions and tell the agency this information.

1. Is there a risk of being assaulted or seriously injured?

2. Do you feel frightened?

3 .Does the abuser have a criminal record? Has the abuser used weapons to attack people in the past?

4. Do you see the abuser on a daily basis?

5. Are you being stalked and constantly harassed?

6. Are you experiencing cyber bullying?

7. Are you feeling suicidal?

8. Are you feeling depressed?

The first three questions relate to your personal safety, the next three questions relate to repeat victimisation and the last three questions relate to your emotional outlook.

Introducing the UK Bullying agencies

Disclaimer: *Listing the following agencies doesn't constitute an endorsement and neither do the following agencies endorse our services.*

Bullies Out

Bullies Out provide help, support and information to individuals, schools, youth and community settings affected by bullying. Bullies Out are a national Charity that provide a range of innovative anti-bullying initiatives and information publications. Although there is no dedicated helpline, Bullies Out provide an Online Mentoring Service which enables those affected by bullying to speak online to a trained mentor in a safe environment.

Using unique interactive workshops, Bullies Out educates children, young people and parents on the effects of bullying, encouraging them to speak out and deal with it effectively. To assist schools with their anti-bullying campaign, the Bullies Out Peer2Peer programme trains young people to become peer mentors enabling them to provide support to the whole school community. ***www.bulliesout.com***

Local Education Authorities and Councils

Within the area in which you live, there will exist different types of programs offered by your local council or your local community safety partnership. Community safety partnerships are usually given the title 'Safer Anytown' for example my community safety partnership is 'Safer Bridgend'. Within this partnership exists an anti-bullying co-ordinator. The standards of service across the UK differ immensely. To find out how to access help in your local area, try using Google and type in word 'bullying' and your community safety partnership. As part of the help given you may be offered, counselling services, restorative justice approaches, education, emotional support and referral to local self-help groups.

Beat Bullying

Beat Bullying programmes are based on peer mentoring and peer activism; encouraging young people to take action against bullying and to help others combat the problem. Each programme focuses on educating young people about bullying issues: what it is, why it happens, what the consequences are, and most importantly, what they can do to stop it. The programmes are flexible in their delivery, and are interactive, encouraging young people to develop their own strategies and solutions to beat bullying.

CyberMentors

CyberMentors is all about kids helping kids online. Young people have the ability to guide and support each other, and this programme helps to empower them to do just that.

CyberMentors are young people aged 11-18 who receive two days intensive face-to-face training from Beatbullying staff which gives them the skills and confidence to mentor offline (in their school or community), online (on the CyberMentors website), and via mobile phones using technology with which they are familiar and enthusiastic about. They then mentor, help, and support other young people from all around the country on issues of bullying, cyberbullying and wellbeing.

As well as mentoring, the CyberMentors programme teaches young people how to safely explore the internet and how to report and handle both cyber and real world bullying.

All online mentoring takes place on the CyberMentors website, which was designed by and for young people, and is moderated both by Beatbullying of staff and qualified counsellors between 8am-2am every day, in addition to leading child protection software that flags up any predatory or abusive behaviour. The site is the only e-mentoring or social networking site to be endorsed by the Child Exploitation and Online Protection Centre (CEOP). There are also Senior CyberMentors (aged 18-25) online who are trained not only to mentor, but also to support CyberMentors in their roles.

Counsellors provide a core part of the support service helping both mentors and mentees. CyberMentors can refer any mentee who has presented with an issue they feel unable to deal with to a counsellor. Counsellors also provide online supervision for all CyberMentors every 3 to 6 months to answer questions and make sure they are all enjoying mentoring others.

To talk about getting your school involved in the CyberMentors programme, please email *diane.lench@beatbullying.org.*

ReSync

The **ReSync** programme is an innovative adaption of the award-winning CyberMentors programme, providing both on and offline mentoring for 14-25 year olds who are moving into education, employment or training. ReSync uses a safe social networking model to support excluded and vulnerable young people with trained mentors, counsellors and advisors, who guide and support disengaged young people and signpost them to specialist help and services where needed.

ReSync Mentors are trained young people from across the UK, which gives them the opportunity to develop and use soft skills to support their peers. As well as having access to support from ReSync Mentors, Advisors and Counsellors for their own needs, they can also refer on young people if they feel that their mentee needs more support. By helping other young people who may be in the same or similar circumstances, ReSync Mentors have the opportunity to make a real difference, which has a significant and positive effect on the well-being, confidence, soft skills, life chances and aspirations of the mentors themselves and those being mentored.

Gateway

Gateway is the name given to Beatbullying's intervention programme that uses therapeutic relationships to achieve positive outcomes for young people. We developed the notion of Gateway to reflect the continuum of behaviour on which some young people find themselves; highly vulnerable to bullying behaviours, influenced negatively by peer pressure, struggling with poor role-modelling or difficulties at home, perhaps already demonstrating anti-social behaviours and a tendency towards criminal activity. We believe that intense intervention work can prevent many of these young people tipping through the 'Gateway' into negative behaviours.

Crisis is an opportunity for change, a chance to improve a young person's way of living, and this is where many of these young people will find themselves in the Gateway project. We invite them into a programme where we have created an atmosphere that is accepting and accommodates change.

Often these young people have placed upon them conditional worth (gang initiation, parental love) from significant people in their lives. In an attempt to protect themselves from upset they go through the process of condemning themselves to a particular life style which prevents them from dreaming or hoping. This is often one of self deprecation and what they believe to be their true potential. Their understanding of what might be an isolated situation that has opportunity for change can become distorted, and this is something Beatbullying's Gateway programme can bring into their awareness and as a result, allow them to live their lives to the full.

Using a combination of three theoretical backgrounds, we look at the thoughts, feelings and behaviours in the conscious and unconscious. We aim to look at each young person as an individual and explore their individual and collective life experiences, and facilitate their journey in assisting them to make sense of what they think, feel and have experienced. The insight of the Gateway programme helps by giving them the opportunity to change (cognitive-behavioural), guiding them towards achieving their individual desires, as well as taking responsibility and ownership of their life choices and the actions they take, giving them meaning from their everyday existence (person-centred).

The aim of this is to work is to bring confusing thoughts, feelings and situations into the conscious and by exploring the results of conflict, help these young people to develop the ability to chose and make informed decisions. We aim for them to gain autonomy and be provided with healthy ways of viewing their world and enhancing their life aspirations. In all cases this is a process that takes time.

LGBT

Beatbullying works with many young people that suffer the indignity and trauma of homophobic bullying. Young people who are questioning their sexuality or identify as lesbian, gay, bisexual or transgendered are often the targets of pernicious harassment and bullying behaviours from their peers. Our LGBT programme has been setup to address the issue and to provide both offline and online support to young people via the CyberMentors programme.

Streetwise is a programme that enables young people to discuss sexual bullying, exploitation and grooming behaviours, and educates young people around healthy and unhealthy relationships, including sexual relationships. The programme is delivered through a number of workshops and utilises a range of different methods. Through the use of discussions, group work, new media and creative sessions, the young people involved explore sexual bullying, sexual exploitation, grooming, healthy relationships, being safe and what it is to be "streetwise".

As with all Beatbullying programmes, Streetwise utilises peer mentoring, but with a particular focus on sexual bullying and healthy relationships. It seeks to raise awareness and educate young people, allowing them to make healthy decisions about their lives, empowering them to be able to handle themselves and situations in an effective manner consequently helping the lives of others.

During the workshops we explore campaigning skills and the group will then use those skills to create a campaign, which we then help them to roll out into their communities. All the materials act as useful resource for young people and professionals working to address the issue of sexual bullying.

Streetwise is designed to meet a range of government agendas, and builds on and complements existing sustainable SRE or PSHE work being done in schools. It offers a safe, non-authoritarian and non-judgemental environment where young people can discuss their experiences and opinions on sensitive issues and the influences (media, peer pressure) exerted on them.

In summary, the programme aims to:

- ❑ Understand the experiences of young people in regards to sexual bullying, and discover the key issues and concerns around relationships

- ❑ Explore how Streetwise can enable young people to discuss sensitive issues, and increase their knowledge and understanding of the issue

- ❑ Provide young people with the skills and confidence to challenge behaviours

- ❑ Enable young people to create potential solutions and strategies for dealing with situations, both helping to keep themselves safe, and others too.

Interfaith

The BB Interfaith approach is one which recognises and celebrates difference and suggests that all faiths should be positively endorsed. The programme encourages young people from all faiths to identify a common humanity, working to reduce and prevent incidents of faith-based bullying, bigotry, sectarianism, and intolerance. By providing an outlet, raising awareness and increasing young people's understands of religious issues – the programme of builds positive relationships and cohesive communities.

The programme embeds the core BBMentoring approach (a form of peer mentoring), but has a particular focus on faith-based and related identity-based issues. These programmes aim to empower young people to make youth-led decisions, take action over their own lives and make positive contributions to their schools and local communities.

In addition to providing support, mentors also become active in developing the wider school and community involvement, through developing a wide range of leadership skills, activism and communication, as well as actively engaging with parents, professionals, decision makers (politicians), and the media at a national and local level. Thus, the project outputs cascade back into the communities in which we are working through our peer education system, led by our newly trained inter-faith anti-bullying ambassadors/leaders. These young leaders will then, as with all Beatbullying's prevention work, have the skills and tools to educate, mentor and support (with the assistance of experts) the next tranche of inter-faith leaders.

The project respects the cultural wishes of differing faiths and offers workshops to groups of girls, groups of boys and mixed gender groups. It takes into account the fact that young people may be becoming increasingly secular and thus do not necessarily have strong, or indeed any, religious views, but still identify as belonging to a particular religious group for family and cultural reasons. Its aim is to encourage people from all backgrounds to work together for the common good and to recognise that behind different background there is a common good and civic identity which binds us all.

In short, the programme aims to:

- ❑ Understand what the key opportunities and challenges are for young people living in a multi-faith society

- ❑ Discover how BB Interfaith can build better understanding between young people with different belief systems, so disagreement and diversity can be discussed openly without conflict, anger or violence

- ❑ Challenging young people to explore different belief and value systems and understanding how they impact young people in relation to living and being at school together

- ❑ Understanding what is the experience of young people in relation to religious and faith-based bullying.

Beat Bullying   www.beatbullying.org

Kidscape

Kidscape is committed to keeping children safe from abuse. Kidscape is the first charity in the UK established specifically to prevent bullying and child sexual abuse. Kidscape believes that protecting children from harm is key.

Kidscape works UK-wide to provide individuals and organisations with practical skills and resources necessary to keep children safe from harm. The Kidscape staff equips vulnerable children with practical non-threatening knowledge and skills in how to keep themselves safe and reduce the likelihood of future harm.

Kidscape works with children and young people under the age of 16, their parents/carers, and those who work with them.

Kidscape offers:

- ❑ A Helpline offering support and advice to parents of bullied children

- ❑ Booklets, Literature, Posters, Training Guides, Educational Videos on bullying, child protection, and parenting

- ❑ National Comprehensive Training Programme on child safety & behaviour management issues

- ❑ Advice and Research

- ❑ Confidence Building Sessions for children who are bullied

Kidscape operates an anti-bullying helpline for parents of bullied children. The number is **08451 205 204**, and advisers are currently available at the following times:
Monday - Thursday: 10am to 4pm
www.kidscape.org.uk

Respect Me Scotland's Anti Bullying Service

Scotland's Anti-bullying Service

respectme, Scotland's Anti-Bullying Service was launched in March 2007. Funded by the Scottish Government and managed in partnership with SAMH (Scottish Association for Mental Health), and LGBT Youth Scotland.

respectme works with all adults who have a role to play in the lives of children and young people to give them the practical skills and confidence to deal with bullying behaviour, wherever it occurs. Free training is provided at events across Scotland and work with organisations at a local and strategic level to develop and review anti-bullying policies and practices.

respectme also campaigns at a national level to traise awareness of bullying behaviour and its impact on children and young people.

respectme is not a helpline - respectme provides practical advice and guidance on developing and reviewing anti-bullying policies and initiatives and identifying the best ways of putting them into practice - but we can put you in touch with other organisations who have trained counsellors you can discuss any worries with.
www.respectme.org.uk

Northern Ireland Anti Bullying Forum

The Northern Ireland Anti-Bullying Forum (NIABF) has a membership of over twenty-five regional statutory and voluntary organisations all acting together to end bullying of children and young people.
www.niabf.org.uk

Peace Mala
"Creative education that empowers
and embraces all
Uniting the World in Peace"

Peace Mala and Hate Crime

Peace Mala is an award winning project for peace that I began in 2001, in response to the racial and religious bullying of pupils in my school that came out of the 9/11 aftermath. What became apparent in those dark days was that fear of difference is often based on the ignorant attitudes of certain people in the community who have grown up believing we all have to conform to the social, cultural or religious 'norms' of the day if we are to be accepted and respected in life. Such misguided attitudes can breed hostility, division and bigotry. If left uncorrected, this can lead on to hate crime.

Peace Mala sets about putting this misunderstanding right by focusing on the Golden Rule with the intention of educating and reminding everyone that this rule is recognised by many scholars, teachers and philosophers. It is also universal to all compassionate faiths. Simply stated, it is:

"Treat others as you would wish them to treat you."

This is the central message of the Peace Mala bracelet. Its intention is to cut through all forms of prejudice, to confront bullying, to support human rights and to celebrate what makes us different from each other. No one has the right to target another with abuse because they are perceived as 'incompatible' with the rules or beliefs of a particular group. Peace Mala reminds us that we all belong and that communities filled with colour and difference make life more interesting and exciting.

The Peace Mala bracelet and project works by using creative and empowering educational activities that embrace and include everyone. Peace Mala is totally inclusive in its approach. With Peace Mala Accreditation for schools, youth groups and community groups, everyone is encouraged to engage in exciting activities which remind us that we are all inter-connected and need each other. There is no room for hate crime.

Pam Evans
Founder of Peace Mala

For more information about Peace Mala explore:
www.peacemala.org.uk
Contact: **info@peacemala.org.uk**
Tel: **01792 774225**
Peace Mala is a non-religious, non-political registered charity.
Registered Charity No: 1118053

Relationship violence agencies

Childline

The UK's free and confidential helpline is not just for children they also help young people in distress or danger. Counsellors provide advice and support, by phone and online, 24 hours a day. You can get help and advice about a wide range of issues, including violence and abuse in your relationship on the ChildLine website. You can also talk to a counsellor online, send ChildLine an email or post on the message boards.

Whatever your worry, it's better out than in.
Helpline: 0800 1111 www.childline.org.uk

Rape Crisis

Rape Crisis Centres offer a range of services for women and girls who have been raped or experienced another form of sexual violence. Rape Crisis Centres are not just for women in 'crisis'. Many women contact them years after they have been raped or sexually abused. You can contact the National Sexual Violence Helpline for help and advice and you can find contact details for your nearest Rape Crisis Centre on Rape Crisis' website.

National helpline: 0808 802 9999 (12pm – 2.30pm and 7pm – 9.30pm)

Broken Rainbow

Broken Rainbow offers support for lesbian, gay, bisexual and transgender (LGBT) people experiencing domestic violence. It also aims to raise awareness in the LGBT community and elsewhere of the impact of homophobic, transphobic and same sex domestic violence on the lives of LGBT people.

Broken Rainbow run a Helpline where operators are highly trained and experienced in the specifics of LGBT domestic violence, with many coming from front line services. They understand the issues you'll face and go through extended training to provide you with the best support they can.

Help line: 03009995428 www.broken-rainbow.org.uk

The Survivors Trust

The Survivors Trust is a charity which works with people who are victims or survivors of rape, sexual violence and childhood sexual abuse. It provides a range of counselling, therapeutic and support services.

The Survivors Trust - 01788 550 554

Emotional support groups

Victim Support

Victim Support offer free and confidential help to victims of crime, their family, friends and anyone else affected. They give information, emotional support and practical help. You don't have to report a crime to the police to get our help and can get support at any time, whenever the crime happened.

Victim Support - 0845 30 30 900

The Samaritans

Samaritans provides confidential non-judgemental emotional support, 24 hours a day for people who are experiencing feelings of distress or despair, including those which could lead to suicide. They are there for you if you're worried about something, feel upset or confused, or just want to talk to someone. You can contact the Samaritans by telephone, email, letter and face to face in most of their branches.

The Samaritans - 08457 90 90 90

Support Line

Support Line provides a confidential telephone helpline offering emotional support to any individual on any issue. The Helpline is primarily a preventative service and aims to support people before they reach the point of crisis. It is particularly aimed at those who are socially isolated, vulnerable, at risk groups and victims of any form of abuse.

Website: **www.supportline.org.uk**
Telephone: 01708 765200
Email: **info@supportline.org.uk**

Hate crime agencies

True Vision

A national scheme supported by all police forces in England, Wales and Northern Ireland providing information to the public about what hate crime is and the ways you can report it. You can report hate crimes through the true vision website.
www.report-it.org.uk/home

Disability and mental health

VOICE UK

A national charity supporting people with learning disabilities and other vulnerable people who have experienced crime or abuse. We also support their families, carers and professional workers. VOICE UK operates a telephone helpline staffed between 9 am and 4 pm Monday, Tuesday and Thursday, 9 am to 12 noon on Wednesday and 10 am to 5 pm on Friday. The helpline number: 080 8802 8686 is displayed on every page on the website. The helpline is also for parents, carers and professional workers. We provide help and information about how to do things, like making a complaint, and what to do if you need help if you are a victim or witness to a crime.

Gypsy, Roma and Traveller

Gypsy Traveller

www.gypsy-traveller.org Advice, information and training organization providing a wide range of services to all Travellers nation wide.

Travellers Times

www.travellerstimes.org.uk News, pictures, video, opinion and resources from within the Gypsy, Roma and Traveller communities.

LGBT

Gender Trust online

The largest Registered Charity (no. 1088150) helping adults throughout the United Kingdom who are Transsexual, Gender Dysphoric, Transgender (i.e. those who seek to adjust their lives to live as women or men, or come to terms with their situation despite their genetic background), or those who's lives are affected by gender identity issues.
Help Line 0845 2310505 www.gendertrust.org.uk

GALOP

Galop works to prevent and challenge homophobic and transphobic hate crime in Greater London. Galop operates a Helpline. This provides advice and support to lesbians, gay men, bisexual and transgender people who have experienced homophobic or transphobic hate crime or violence in the greater London area. It is free and you can remain anonymous if you wish.

Galop can advise on the law and your rights and give you advice on immediate and practical steps you can take to deal with LGBT hate crime you may be experiencing. Galop does not provide counselling but we can refer you to other LGBT-friendly organisations who offer more specialised services.

Advocate on your behalf with the police or other organisations

If you have already reported an incident to the police or another organisation and are unhappy with their response or feel you need further assistance, Galop can liaise for you to try and resolve the situation.

Report a crime to the police on your behalf

If you have experienced or know of any anti-LGBT hate crime or incident but do not feel able to report this directly to the police, Galop can do this for you and act as an intermediary if you want the incident to be investigated further. You can remain anonymous if you wish, although if you want us to liaise with the police on your behalf we will need to be able to contact you. You can use our Online Report Form or phone our Shoutline.

Help you to obtain Criminal Injuries Compensation

If you have received injuries as a result of a violent homophobic or transphobic hate crime, Galop can advise you and assist with the process of applying for and claiming financial compensation through the Criminal Injuries Compensation system.

Provide you with details of LGBT-friendly solicitors and police officers

Many London boroughs now have dedicated or part-time LGBT Liaison Officers who can be more sympathetic if you experienced a homophobic or transphobic incident. Galop can put you in touch with the appropriate officer in your area or liaise with them on your behalf. If you need further legal help Galop can also give you details of solicitors or other legal representatives who specialise or regularly take LGBT cases.

Make a complaint against the police

The Metropolitan Police now have a comprehensive policy to ensure that they provide a fair and unbiased service to anyone who experiences hate-crime in London. If you do not feel that you have received correct treatment from the police, Galop can tell you the minimum standards of service you can expect and help you to make a formal complaint if this is appropriate. Visit our Help With The Police page for more information.

020 7704 2040 www.galop.org.uk

Albert Kennedy Trust

Albert Kennedy Trust website supporting lesbian, gay, bisexual and trans homeless young people.

Every day we deal with the effects homelessness can have on young people's lives. With your help we can do so much more to support young homeless people in our community. This service is only available in London and Manchester.
www.akt.org.uk

Imaan

Imaan supports LGBT Muslim people, their families and friends, to address issues of sexual orientation within Islam. It provides a safe space and support network to address issues of common concern through sharing individual experiences and institutional resources.

020 3393 5188 www.imaan.org.uk

Lesbian and Gay Foundation

The Lesbian & Gay Foundation provides more direct services and resources to more lesbian, gay and bisexual people than any other charity of its kind in the UK.

0845 3 30 30 30

London Lesbian and Gay Switchboard

London Lesbian & Gay Switchboard provides a range of services for the lesbian, gay, bisexual and transgender (LGBT) community.

The services include our helpline, online chat through instant messaging, email support, information on sexual health and the Turing Network database, a public access search facility that enables anyone to look for support or services catering for the LGBT community.

Whatever way you choose to contact us, our fully trained volunteers will be there to help and can offer you support and information on any subject to do with sexuality.

Our volunteers are helpful, friendly and supportive, and every one of them identifies as either lesbian, gay or bisexual.

You don't have to be lesbian, gay or bisexual to contact us – we talk to friends, parents and family members too.

Why contact us?

I'm coming out... – Call us if you want to talk about your feelings, are frightened, confused or isolated.

I'm going out... – We can give you listings and details of bars, clubs, saunas, social and sports groups and support groups. We can also tell you what's going on and where in the rest of the UK.

I'm staying in... – Ask us anything you like about sex: wanting sex, having sex, safer sex, sexual health and where to go if you have an itch or a sore. If you're worried about HIV and AIDS, we can tell you what the risks are and what precautions you can take.

Oh, by the way – no matter how you choose to contact us, this is what we won't do:

- ❑   We won't tell you what to do

- ❑   We won't judge you

❏ We won't tell anyone else about what you talk or write about

Our Helpline 020 7837 7324

Transgender

Gender Identity Research and Education Society

GIRES has an online facility to report transphobic hate crime available at tcrime.net. Details a number of support groups across the UK.
www.gires.org.uk

Stonewall

A charity that campaigns on issues affecting lesbian, gay and bisexual people. Has a number of publications and interesting articles www.stonewall.org.uk
08000502020

Race or religion

The Community Security Trust (CST)

CST (Community Security Trust) is proud of Britain's diverse and vibrant Jewish community, and seeks to protect its many achievements from the external threats of bigotry, antisemitism and terrorism.

CST provides physical security, training and advice for the protection of British Jews. CST assists victims of antisemitism and monitors antisemitic activities and incidents. CST represents British Jewry to Police, Government and media on antisemitism and security.

CST believes that the fight against antisemitism and terrorism is an integral part of safeguarding our wider democratic British society against extremism and hatred.

London Head Office - Telephone: 020 8457 9999

Emergency 24 hour pager: 07659 101 668

Email: enquiries@thecst.org.uk

Manchester and Northern Regions - Telephone: 0161 792 6666

Emergency 24 hour pager: 0800 980 0668

www.thecst.org.uk

The Monitoring Group

The Monitoring Group offers a helpline service has been a essential for victims of racial violence. In addition to the ongoing support, case work is managed in a professional manner.

0800 374 618

Muslim Line

The Muslim Line is a UK based initiative arranged to help Muslims that have suffered from a hate crime due to their race, ethnic background or religion in public or at work.

The aims and objectives of the Muslim Line are as follows:

Advice and Guidance

We advise the caller as to whether the incident is a hate crime and guide him/her to other organisations that we feel can provide help through support and counselling. In case of emergencies and with the prior permission of the caller, we will call 999 on his/her behalf.

Sympathetic Ear

A supportive member of our staff will answer all calls and provide as much confidential emotional support, help and time to the caller as possible.

Confidentiality

The caller's details are treated with the utmost confidence and no information is divulged without the caller's prior permission.

Let us support you. Call the Muslim Line in complete confidentiality:
0845 22 50 50 2 (calls charged at local rate)
Tel 0208 840 4840
Fax 0208 840 8819

THE
PSYCHOLOGY
OF
BULLYING
AND
HATECRIME

We are taught within schools that bullying is a range of behaviours. We all know what bullying looks like, we know the effect. We know that bullies punish others, but why? Would it not be useful to understand why?

In the many years of speaking to many bullies, I've come to realise that the simplicity presented to you, is somewhat confusing. We use the word 'bully' to categorise a person and a particular behaviour. This method of association is an easy method, it gives a particular predetermined answer to an age old problem. 'John' shouted at me and then hit me, he is therefore a bully. This view point is fixed and stagnant. We are assuming that a 'bully' is always going to be a 'bully'. Are you always going to be a victim? Perhaps a more rounded balanced view would account for the ability for others to change.

But who is John?

Emotions

Is 'John' his emotions? What emotion was John feeling when he hit you? Was he angry? Was he sad? Was he anxious? Was he frightened?

Ego

Who does John think he is? Does he think he's clever? Does he think he is special? Is John self-important and selfish?

Needs and wants

What does John want? What does John need? Does he seek attention? Does he seek power? Is he happy? Is he sad? Does he seek belonging? Does he enjoy punishment?

Morale compass

Is he always getting into trouble? Does he have any boundaries? Does he know the difference between right and wrong?

Emotional intelligence

How does he think? Is he rigid or flexible? Can he problem solve? Can he see others points of view? Can he understand your feelings? Can he empathise? Can he understand his own feelings?

Relationships

How does he communicate? Do his words and his body language match? Does he have strained relationships? Is he a calm person?

Support

Do his parents support him? Does he have parents? Does he have guidance? How is John supported? Does he drink alcohol? Does he take drugs?

The person that you see in front of you, who you know as 'John' the 'bully'. Is really 'John' and his emotions, his ego, his needs and wants, his moral compass, his emotional intelligence, his inner relationship and his support network. At a deeper level of thinking the reason why John is behaving the way he does is due to one key point.

John's inner world is not in balance, the way John thinks, feels, relates, emphasises, communicates and behaves is dysfunctional. Johns thinking mind and his emotional awareness are in conflict, and it is this conflict and frustration, that drives his behaviour.

John's external world may also be dysfunctional.

The following descriptions are not are not excuses for behaviour, it is always the thinking mind and blind emotional reactions that drive bullying behaviour. However, cause-and-effect operates at all levels and the following descriptions may heighten and add to irrational thinking and emotive behaviour and therefore build upon the bullying or hate encounter.

John may have suffered a recent bereavement within his family. John's parents may be going through a violent divorce. John may have a problem with alcohol and drugs. John has been brought up in abusive household. John has un-diagnosed psychiatric problems. John is part of a gang. John is hungry all the time. John doesn't understand what a normal relationship is. John has been abused all throughout his life. John's brother committed suicide. John's dad is in jail and his mother can't cope. John feels angry, John doesn't get supported, and John failed at school. The media are promoting all types of excuses.

Bullying is punishment.

When we consider the types of bullying behaviour, we may come to realise that bullying is a form of punishment. Why do people feel the need to punish others? Where do our ideas of punishment come from? Who has the right to punish others? What is the difference between punishment and the consequence of behaviour?

The world English dictionary defines:

> ## 'Punishment'
> *1. A penalty or sanction given for any crime or offence.*

There are many laws described by parliament and throughout history society has made it clear that certain crimes are punishable. It is generally agreed that the following natural laws uphold society's peace and happiness.

- ❏ Making the intention to promote non-violence and avoiding activities that cause physical harm to others. For example; walking away from the threat of hostility and helping others avoid the threat of violence.

- ❏ Making the intention to be truthful and avoiding dishonesty. For example acting in a way that accurately details the facts of an experience, instead of exaggerating and covering up the facts in the anticipation of a reward of some kind or blaming another because of the fear of punishment.

- ❏ Making the intention to promote positive relationships with others and avoiding behaviour that involves sexual misconduct and family breakdown. For example maintaining faithfulness and avoiding opportunities that could place faithfulness in jeopardy.

- ❏ Making the intention to use proper speech that is quiet and peaceful and allows communication to flourish. Avoiding speech that is loud, hostile, aggressive and problematic. For example speaking when we are calm, and avoiding speech that is fuelled by the emotions of anxiety, anger and malice.

- ❏ Making the intention to share our time, resources, money, friendship, ability and knowledge for the benefit of others. Avoiding activities that foster a strong sense of 'me' and 'I' and therefore interfere with cooperation, interdependence and community support.

- ❏ Respecting others property. For example avoiding reckless or intentional criminal damage.

Across all cultures, it is widely accepted that when a person physically harms another human being, acts dishonestly, engages in sexual misconduct, speaks harshly in public about others and damages others personal property. An act of punishment has to follow this particular pattern of destructive behaviour. The only person within western society who has the power to decide what type of punishment should follow by law is a 'Judge'. Notice that the descriptions of these offences are particularly serious in nature. At the community level many people impose punitive means on others, for example, parents, teachers, police officers, enforcement officers etc.

Development of the abusive personality

In the next set of paragraphs, I want you to really consider the abuser's thinking patterns. The next couple of chapters may be an explanation as to why abusive people share some of the same behaviours and often use the same tactics. I want you to think of the abuser as the developmental child.

Whilst the abuser was growing up in his/her childhood, they were probably introduced to a simple form of ethics by the use of reward or punishment. If they showed positive behaviour, they were usually rewarded. For example, if the child did what their parents asked, went to sleep, spoke nicely to their parents, shared their sweets, the child was usually given a reward for such good behaviour. This type of conditioning is evident across many schools today and it is perceived as a successful way of allowing young children to understand rule setting, standards and general etiquette.

Rewards are followed with positive affirmations *"You were such a good boy."*
You cleaned your teeth, your parent said, *"That's good."*
You listened, your parent said, *"That's good."*
You shared with others, your parent said, *"That's good, well done."*
You passed your exams, your parent said, *"That's good."*
You had a wash, your parent said, *"That's good."*
You eat all your food, your parent said, *"That's good."*

How does the abuser become so judgemental? Reward and punishment

Notice that everyday activities have 'good' affirmations. With such obvious labelling, does the word 'good' have meaning in different circumstances? This process confuses the abuser as a child. The concept of 'good' is not used within its proper context. Every individual has their own perception of the meaning of 'good'. Continually throughout the days, months and years of child development behaviour is conditioned with the reward of something pleasant for right, good and proper behaviour. On the opposing side, when a child acts against the common standard an appropriate punishment is administered. Punishment is a matter of perception. For some it could be a firm "No", for others it could mean to be ridiculed, embarrassed, beaten and harassed.

The child wasn't taught to problem solve.

It is at the stage where problems begin to surface. For every action there needs to be an equal and opposite reaction. For example when a child does something wrong the decision to punish or spell out the consequences of an action needs to be considered from four perspectives.

1. Is the action or behaviour morally wrong? To determine if an action is morally wrong, we need to ask two questions. Has the action caused inner pain and discomfort to the person 'doing' the action? Has the action caused pain and discomfort to the person 'receiving'?

For example, when a child develops an outburst of intense anger the child from the inner perspective experiences disharmony, discomfort and internal stress. Inner experience of anger is a form of discomfort to the person 'doing' or 'experiencing anger'. The person on the receiving end also experiences pain and discomfort, the inner emotional drive of anger creates a behaviour change that results in the receiving of violence and hostility. Receiving of violence causes the person to feel emotionally targeted and physically injured.

The child that is 'doing' may experience a consequence of anger. Anger's inner feeling creates disharmony and there is no peace within the child. The other children within the school or group may notice that the child has a problem with anger. The awareness of anger creates distance between people, groups and communities. The angry child may be excluded from certain activities, may feel lonely, may feel considerably stressed, friendships will deteriorate and opportunities for sharing, building relationships and having fun will end.

2. Having considered if an action or behaviour is morally wrong, am I justified in doing something about this problem?

3. Having witnessed this behaviour, what options do I have that may be proportional to addressing this problem?

4. Is the use of punishment necessary, in this set of circumstances? What can the child learn from this experience? What is the child prepared to do to make amends and restore peace and harmony within the context of the relationship?

How does the abusive child become confused?

These four questions, open up the whole idea of punishment and introduce a thought process that considers the moral question. Moving away from punishment, we learn to consider a moral problem from the perspective of calmness, learning and proportional responses. This is a problem solving approach.

Such a simple question, but rarely considered by many. From a human perspective with the absence of religious thinking, what does it mean to be good? Who decides to set the rules of 'good' and 'bad'? The answer to this question is mixed. Rule setting generally begins with our parents, families, siblings, role models, education, religious upbringing, media, institutions, governments and societal pressures. What would happen if some of these influences got the concept wrong? What if the controlling parent didn't consider the four moral questions?

"You ate all your food, you can have your pudding as you are a good child."

"You listened at school and your teacher says you are well behaved, you deserved your stars and I have bought you a toy for your good example."

Based on this small example, rules begin to form and the dividing line between 'good' and 'bad' start to form. The word or concept 'good' pairs with a 'reward' and this creates a sense of 'wanting'.

Bullying is common in classrooms around the world: About 15 percent of children are victimized, leading to depression, anxiety, loneliness, and other negative outcomes. What's driving bullies to behave the way they do? According to a new large-scale Dutch study, most bullies are motivated by the pursuit of status and affection.

The word or concept 'bad' pairs with 'punishment' and this creates a sense of 'avoiding'.

Let's suppose the abuser was brought up in a strict household where 'punishment' was administered more than reward. Remember the abuser is a fanatical extremist, favouring punishment more so than reward. The abuser does not understand calmness, communication, reparation and justice.

Punishment causes further problems

When the abuser broke the code, rule, standard or law, they were given an appropriate punishment. Affirmations such as 'you're naughty' or a 'bad child' were placed upon them. Some families use fear as a tactic. For example taking away a privilege, threatening to do something horrible or even using a slap as physical punishment. Now suppose that the abuser stole something because they were hungry. The consequences of being caught were always met with physical punishment. They always had a 'back hand'. The fear of being hit, did not stop them from actually stealing, it was ineffective. Now suppose that they got caught red handed. Are they honestly going to tell the truth? The abuser knows that even if they tell the truth, they're still going to be physically punished. Would it be OK to limit the story, perhaps to blame someone else, lessen the blow and save their skin? Fear doesn't promote honesty, in fact it can support the habit of dishonesty. The abuser as a child learns to become engrossed in the habit of dishonesty and lives in a world of denial. The child does this because they want to avoid punishment. **As an adult abuser, when confronted with the facts of abuse, the abuser knows at a subconscious level that 'abusive behaviour' should be punished, because it is 'bad', but the feeling of 'bad' involves 'avoiding'. As an adult there is no one to impose this rule so they never admit it to themselves and lie. They blame you, because they learnt at an early age that dishonesty stopped them from receiving punishment.**

In families where there is continued punishment, no one in the household has any say in this process. The abuser imposes rigid ideas onto the family members. These ideas are unbalanced, the abuser will always sway to the punishment side of 'bad' behaviour. Whilst the abuser imposes there is always an emotional component and this component involves fear and anxiety. The anxiety that a child feels becomes related with the judgements of 'bad'. The abuser has a highly confused system of what is 'good or bad' and this creates havoc within the family's system of ethics and relationships with others. Family members, where there is unbalanced 'splitting', experience punishment for the smallest of activities.

Children and adolescents who lack social problem-solving skills are more at risk of becoming bullies, victims or both than those who don't have these difficulties, says new research published by the American Psychological Association. The imposed splitting experience doesn't allow the development of early problem solving skills. The child's view is either 'good' or 'bad'.

This is how the dysfunction begins. The child receives punishment for very minor activities. For example:

You did not clean your teeth, your parent 'threatens punishment or punishes' the abuser as the child connects this feeling with anxiety.

You did not listen, your parent 'threatens punishment or punishes' the abuser as the child connects this feeling with anxiety.

You did not share with others, your parent 'threatens punishment or punishes' the abuser as the child connects this feeling with anxiety.

You did not revise for your exams, your parent 'threatens punishment or punishes' the abuser as the child connects this feeling with anxiety.

Child says, "I feel sad and upset", the parent says, "It's bad to feel sad" and threatens punishment. For example, "I will put you on the naughty step."

You did not wash your hands, your parent 'threatens punishment or punishes'.

You did not eat all your food, your parent 'threatens punishment or punishes'.

The concept of rules and punishment couple with negative emotions.

Notice that at this point the child as the abuser has no ability to make sense of a minor discrepancy; the rules of punishment are enforced. The world view of the child is enforced. This level of punishment and relationship with the feeling of anxiety causes even more problems. At a later time, usual activities become linked with the feeling of anxiety. The type of punishment that is used within the home includes:

- ❏ Using force, a slap or a push
- ❏ Threatening that 'bad' things will happen
- ❏ Criticising weakness
- ❏ Comparing others
- ❏ Grounding or locking in a room
- ❏ Controlling access and friendship

Eating certain foods, playing with certain friends, choosing certain activities, dressing a certain way. These examples are just simply choices, but they get incorrectly judged from a moral standpoint. Think back to 'John', can you begin to see how his emotions, his ego, his needs and wants, his moral compass, his emotional intelligence, his inner relationship and his support network could begin to deteriorate.

It's all about inner and outer control

As the child encounters experiences that differ from his/her set of rules or good affirmations a predictable response emerges. When the child sees or experiences an opposing set of circumstances, the term 'bad' resonates. The word 'bad' moves into a whole myriad of feelings. Feelings that we don't like and compel us to act in ways that foster aversion, blame and denial. Our view imposes on others and our behaviour changes. The abuser has a highly conditioned anxiety complex and whenever the abuser experiences the opposing set of circumstances, anxiety increases. **The abuser cannot cope with anxiety and so must control you, because the abuser believes that you are the cause of their personal anxiety. The abuser projects those inner feelings onto you.**

That person is fat, 'that's bad, feeling anxious'.

That person doesn't have clean shoes, 'that's bad, feeling anxious'.

That person hasn't combed her hair, 'that's bad, feeling anxious'.

Literally, the abuser as the child begins to see the world as 'bad'. The inner process of splitting develops at a subconscious level and begins to create a thinking pattern that is notoriously judgemental and deluded in many ways. The feeling of anxiety becomes associated with 'splitting'.

Reward and punishment are effective means when used in the correct circumstances.

The effects of living with an abusive personality "the extremes of reward and punishment".

- ❑ When a family member doesn't get a reward for acting in a good and benevolent way. How do you think they feel? Do you think that they may feel disappointed when they don't get a reward? The feeling of not being rewarded is in essence a feeling of 'frustration'. The repeated feeling of frustration can lead to a feeling of injustice. The child may lose motivation and avoids trying to act in a beneficial way. The child thinks "Why bother, I never get noticed or rewarded for trying?" Repeated and systematic external control (the abusive parent) can lead towards the idea of being a victim. This is what happens in an abusive home. The child thinks "This is happening because of me, I am to blame" or "I am always getting treated this way, and it is so unfair". The child's observation is actually correct, they are being targeted by this process. The inner feeling of disappointment then links with the thinking process of trying to be good or benevolent. This conditioned process is harmful because of two reasons. The child can become apathetic and begins to learn to 'fail' when engaged in any activity. This reinforces the view that the abuser has imposed on them. Continued learnt 'failure' results in even more 'failure'. Because the feeling of disappointment and frustration is particularly emotionally powerful, the child avoids activities that are particularly benevolent or helpful. These two forces are at work and are harmful, learnt failure and an absence of helpful behaviours. This can easily be seen in children.

- ❑ From the opposite side of the spectrum. A belief of entitlement may also begin to form. For example, the abuser as a child says to another child "I gave you some of my sweets and therefore I am entitled to some of yours" or "I did what you asked and therefore I am entitled to a reward". What happens when your child's belief of entitlement becomes compromised? They don't get what they believe that they deserved and once again inner frustration begins to fester. Where this approach falters is that doesn't develop a coping mechanism or technique when life becomes challenging. When someone hurts us or doesn't reward us. We say "He/she is a bad person!" We project our inner feelings onto that person and make them faulty. We do this because we identify with the idea of 'bad'. We know that 'bad' always with links with 'punishment'. So we decide to punish the other person or make a judgement. Punishment may be administered by gossip, threats, intimidation or the use of violence.

- ❑ Rewards can be used to emotionally blackmail children. The abuser can use the anticipation of rewards as a lever to manipulate and control children. "If you smack your mother and call her names, I will buy you a new bike and then you will be my favourite girl, I love you so much." This manipulative technique creates a sense of guilt mixed with reward and is particularly nasty. When has love ever had a relationship with hitting your mother? This type of manipulation sends the wrong message to children. Love has no relationship with imposed violence.

- ❑ The anticipation of a reward of some kind creates a sense of urgency. The child begins to think "When I receive a reward I will be happy and contented and the inner frustration will go away, I need a reward". Anticipation of punishment creates thinking patterns of aversion. The child begins to plan and worry, plan and worry about the future. In an abusive household 'reward' and 'punishment' move back and forth with lightning speed. The child is caught between opposite poles. When our thinking patterns move from opposing poles, we miss our actual real-world experience. Our children are never in the present moment. Watching children play, we notice how consumed, so in the moment they play. Their surroundings are unimportant, play flows with ease. The anxious child doesn't play with ease, constantly looking for appreciation and worrying about their behaviour. Anxious children lose their childhood.

- ❑ When a family member is confronted with an experience that is deemed as 'bad' (from their point of reference). What happens? For example, suppose in your home it is wrong and bad to walk through the house with wellingtons. The punishment for this offence is simple. A slap across the head. When a child has friends visiting after school time, one of the children walks across the room with wellingtons. The child, on seeing this behaviour, will immediately feel anxious. The anxious feeling is related to the anticipation of punishment. Even though your child will not be punished by witnessing this action, still there remains anxiety. This is a significant burden that has been imposed on a child. It has parallels with why when people see a coiled rope on the floor, they immediately become frightened. They think that they have seen a snake! Emotional drives are far more powerful than our sense of sight.

❑ The conditioned use of the word 'bad' has been overused and becomes mainstream for feelings of loneliness, despair, worry, anxiety, depression, sadness, low mood, apathy, etc. Different feelings have different levels of intensity and duration. When we are in tune with our inner feelings, we become aware of each emotion. This awareness allows us to correctly identify each passing emotion. This can really help us put emotions into perspective. Instead of thinking 'bad, bad, bad'. We can think 'low mood, it will pass'. This is far more gentle and appropriate in the circumstances. This becomes difficult when someone else is telling us how we should feel. Extreme reward and punishment teach children to become emotionally illiterate.

I am not saying that reward and punishment are not suitable in certain situations. For example, a child being punished for hitting another child or being rewarded for sharing with others.

In summary

The following table summarises how repeated and conditioned punishment on behalf of the parent, conditions the child as an abuser. The abusive child becomes dysfunctional and exhibits many contradicting thinking and emotional patterns. The dysfunctional child's environment may provide even more stimulus and condition further negative behaviours. The splitting process manipulates the child's thinking patterns. The result is clear to see bullying at home, at school, within relationships, on the street and at the workplace.

> *The thought manifests as the word*
> *The word manifests as the concept and couples with our emotions*
> *The concept develops into a habit*
> *The habit becomes the character trait or personality*
> *The personality becomes dysfunctional*

Severe and repeated conditioned Punishment at home includes ▼	The Child learns and becomes ▼	The Dysfunctional Child then exhibits ▼	Bullying and Hate Crime Behaviors ▼	Victim's Experience ▼
Severe punishment for breaking minor rules.	Learned helplessness. Fails at tasks to avoid punishment. Child doesn't know how to communicate.	Child feels constantly anxious, doesn't know if they broke the rules or achieved expectations.	Person begins to imposes the rules on others. Assaults people. Damages property.	Receives injuries and feels scared. Always treading on egg shells.
Slapping and hitting	Blames others or lie to avoid physical punishment.	Learns dishonesty as a coping mechanism.	Consistent Liar.	Has to justify the incident and may not be believed.
Sarcasm	Child learns to use harsh words instead of physical contact.	Uses other means to target someone.	Threatening, abusive, cyber bullying.	Feels self-conscious and threatened.
Negative affirmations	Child attributes negativity to all that they do.	Feels depressed and lonely.	Feels depressed at risk of suicide. Feelings of Anxiety.	Begins to believe in negative affirmations. Negativity is contagious.
Emotional Blackmail	Mixed up belief and emotional ideas. You can hit someone when you love them.	Confused belief system.	Sever frustration and inner confusion.	Becomes emotionally sensitive and confused.
Grounding	You have the right to control someone when they have broken the rules.	Jails friends and people who are in a relationship with them.	Controls partners, stalking behavior and jailing.	Manipulated and trapped.
Sanctions	Consistent anxiety, I need to please everyone and I will then get rewarded.	Imposes ideas onto others. Lack of communication.	Inability to communicate. Extremism and imposing behavio.r	Lack of expression and freedom of speech.
Reward or punishment	Child splits every experience into 'good' or 'bad'. Becomes Emotionally illiterate. Doesn't understand feelings.	Judgmental, lack of problem solving skills.	Lack of problem solving skills. Becomes involved in Criminality.	Becomes punished for every action. Creating a feeling of injustice and anxiousness. May feel suicidal.

Remember 'Support'

Make a **S**afety Plan.
Understand that it is not your fault.
Preserve evidence, write about your experiences.
Protect yourself legally; take advice from civil and criminal solicitors.
Apply for a non-molestation order or a restraining order.
Organise support from many agencies; many people can help you.
Respect your health; it will help you keep strong.
Talk to someone; express your feelings.

All personal safety products listed within this book can be purchased from *www.talkandsupport.co.uk*

Bullied Publications also produce two further books:

Safe 'Your complete guide to domestic abuse'.

Morale Matter 'A police officers guide to reducing stress and improving morale in the workplace'.